the
LINDISFARNE
icon

D0177172

Moorlands College Library (MC)

MC63215

Angela Newton
July 2005

the
LINDISFARNE
icon

ST CUTHBERT AND THE 21ST CENTURY
CHRISTIAN

HELEN JULIAN CSF

Text copyright © Helen Julian CSF 2004
The author asserts the moral right
to be identified as the author of this work

Published by
The Bible Reading Fellowship
First Floor, Elsfield Hall
15–17 Elsfield Way, Oxford OX2 8FG

ISBN 1 84101 322 6
First published 2004
10 9 8 7 6 5 4 3 2 1 0
All rights reserved

Acknowledgments
Scripture quotations are taken from The New Revised Standard Version
of the Bible, Anglicized Edition, copyright © 1989, 1995 by the Division
of Christian Education of the National Council of the Churches of Christ
in the USA, and are used by permission. All rights reserved.

Extracts from *The Age of Bede* (chs. 1—46) translated by J.F. Webb
(Penguin Classics, 1965) translation copyright © J.F. Webb, 1965,
Introduction and Notes copyright © D.H. Farmer, 1983, 1988.
Reproduced by permission of Penguin Books Ltd.

A catalogue record for this book is available from the British Library

Printed and bound in Great Britain by
Bookmarque, Croydon

CONTENTS

CHAPTER 1

'A READY PATH TO VIRTUE'

Cynewulf slipped out of the church as soon as the prior gave the blessing. Some of the other monks would stay there to pray; others would go to the small huts which were their cells, to read. Cynewulf, however, was the monastery's cook, and so he left the church and made his way towards the kitchen. There was no wind—unusual for this island monastery—and in the grey light of dawn a thin mist hung over everything. It was a bit eerie, and Cynewulf started as he thought he saw, out of the corner of his eye, a bit of the mist moving. He laughed at himself. That's what came of reading too many lives of the saints, with all their tales of demons.

But this shadow in the mist was very real—flesh and blood. The Vikings had come to Lindisfarne, and Cynewulf was their first victim. His scream of terror brought the other monks tumbling out of the church, out of the huts scattered around. Unarmed and unused to fighting, they were no match for the Viking warriors. In a short time many lay dead or wounded, and the monastery had been stripped of its treasures.

It was 8 June 793. As news of the outrage spread, it shocked everyone who heard it. Alcuin, a deacon, scholar and teacher from York, lamented:

It is nearly 350 years since we and our fathers inhabited this most lovely land. It was not thought that such an invasion from the sea was possible. The church of St Cuthbert is spattered with the blood of the priests of

God, stripped of all its furnishings, exposed to the plundering of pagans —a place more sacred than any other in Britain.[1]

How did this small semi-island off the Northumberland coast become such a sacred place? The clue is in the name of the saint whose church was there—Cuthbert. Cuthbert was a monk, prior of the monastery of Lindisfarne, then a hermit, devoting himself to a life of prayer. He was called away from this life to be bishop of the diocese of Lindisfarne for a short time, before returning to his hermitage, where he died in 687. He was immensely popular in his lifetime, with people travelling from great distances to see him. They came to hear his preaching, ask his advice or to seek for healing; and his death didn't change this. His tomb in the monastery church became a shrine, a place of pilgrimage.

After the first Viking raid, the surviving monks remained on Lindisfarne and pilgrimages resumed, but the threat continued to be present, and it was probably in response to this danger that Ecgred, who was bishop of Lindisfarne between 830 and 845, moved Cuthbert's body to Norham on the River Tweed for a time.

Why was Cuthbert's body so important? We need to know something of the beliefs behind the early medieval cult of the saints and their relics to understand this. Fundamental was the belief that the saint was not only in heaven with God but also still present in his or her earthly remains. Prayers made close to the shrine were therefore especially powerful. The epitaph placed on the tomb of St Martin of Tours in the fourth century expresses this belief very clearly: 'Here lies Martin the bishop, of holy memory, whose soul is in the hand of God; but he is fully here, present and made plain in miracles of every kind.'[2]

It is not surprising, then, that some time later, after Cuthbert's body had been returned to Lindisfarne and the Vikings were again threatening, another bishop of Lindisfarne took his body and set off on wanderings which eventually brought Cuthbert to Chester-le-Street, six miles north of Durham. For seven years from 875, a small community of monks, with the bishop and Eadred, abbot of Carlisle, moved around the north of England and the south of Scotland. They reached the coast of Cumbria and planned to sail across to Ireland, but evidently the saint disapproved. The waves that washed into the boat turned to blood, so they abandoned their plan. Instead they went to Whithorn, and then turned south and stayed for a few months in Crayke in Yorkshire. Finally, in 882, they arrived in Chester-le-Street, where they built a church and a new shrine for Cuthbert.

They stayed here peacefully for over a century, but in 995 there was yet another threat from Vikings, and they fled to Ripon. They started to return to Chester-le-Street, but on the way turned aside to Durham, where they settled permanently. Cuthbert's body is still in Durham, in the great Norman cathedral that replaced the Saxon stone cathedral, which had itself replaced the wooden church built by Cuthbert's community when they arrived there.

Why Durham? Well, the story has it that this was Cuthbert's choice of resting place. The *History of the Church of Durham*, almost certainly written by Symeon, a monk at Durham in the early twelfth century, tells us that on the way back to Chester-le-Street, the cart on which Cuthbert's body was being carried became impossible to move. The bishop, Ealdhun, ordered a three-day vigil, with fasting, and it was during this period that one of the monks, Eadmer, had a revelation that Cuthbert wished to rest at Durham.

Three hundred years after his death, Cuthbert was obviously still a very real presence to the community that travelled with him and finally settled with him in Durham. His presence was felt to be very strong at his shrine behind the high altar in the new cathedral, which became one of the most important centres of pilgrimage in England and remained so until the Reformation. In fact, devotion to Cuthbert was 'reputed to be the greatest hindrance to the course of the English Reformation'.[3] A book written at the end of the 16th century describes the splendours of the shrine just before the Reformation swept away its riches and the monks themselves.

It was made of green marble, decorated with gold, and had a fine covering, scarlet inside and gilded and painted outside. On the top was fine carving, and on one of the ropes by which it was raised and lowered were six silver bells, to let the people know when the cover was lifted up.

Cuthbert had come a long way from the simplicity of minding sheep by the River Leader, in what is now the Scottish borders, but that is where his story starts. All that we know of Cuthbert's life comes from two biographies—one by a monk of Lindisfarne and one (in two versions, poetry and prose) by the Venerable Bede. Both were written within a generation of Cuthbert's death in 687; the monk of Lindisfarne wrote his book around 700, and Bede his verse Life in 716, the prose version following around 721. Neither tells us much about his early life, and his parents go unmentioned, but we know that he had a foster mother, Kenswith, of whom he was very fond and whom he still visited and helped later in his life. The fact that he had a foster mother may mean that he came from a well-to-do family, as these families often fostered their children to another household as part of their education—or it may simply mean that his own family were unable to look after him.

Cuthbert seems to have been an energetic child: the first vivid story about him in Bede's Life pictures him at the age of eight as a boy who 'loved games and pranks... naturally agile and quick-witted and usually won the game'.[4] As he grew older, though, he also began to take his faith seriously. Christianity was relatively new to Britain. Some of the Romans had been Christians, and they had made converts among the native British. When the Romans left, early in the fifth century, many of the institutions of the towns (which seem to have been the strongest centres of Christianity) left with them. Scattered groups of British Christians did remain, however, especially in the marginal western and northern areas where the pagan Saxon incursions of the fifth century had less influence.

It was only when Augustine arrived from Rome, sent by Pope Gregory in 597, that a serious effort was made to evangelize Britain. At around the same time, Irish missionaries, already converted from Rome, began to move into Britain, initially to the monastery on the island of Iona off the west coast of Scotland, and then to the mainland. So there were two sources of faith, both stemming initially from Rome, but one coming via Canterbury and spreading up from the south of England, and the other coming via Ireland and the north-west. Cuthbert, born around 634 in what is now the Scottish borders, was probably influenced by both streams. We don't know whether his parents were Christian but, if so, they were likely to have been first-generation and may have been converted after Cuthbert was born. Faith was still new and fragile in the earlier part of the seventh century.

In whatever way he came to it, Cuthbert had faith. After the few stories of his childhood, we next find him as a shepherd around the River Leader, a stream that runs into the River Tweed. It was a job offering plenty of solitude, and he would pray, especially at night when the other shepherds were asleep. It was while praying one night that he saw something that changed his life. The darkness of the night was lit up by streams of light, and he had a vision of angels escorting a bright human soul to heaven. The next day he heard that Aidan, a monk from Iona who had become the bishop of Lindisfarne, had died the previous night, and Cuthbert knew that it was his soul he had seen. Cuthbert determined to become a monk himself.

Wasting no time, he set off to the monastery at Melrose. He had a horse and a spear, which would suggest that he was not poor. Before he came to the gate of the monastery, though, he dismounted and gave his horse and spear to a servant, so that he arrived on foot and unarmed. The prior, Boisil, received him kindly, and when the abbot Eata (later bishop of Lindisfarne) arrived, Cuthbert was admitted as a novice. His hair was cut into the Celtic tonsure, shaved back from his forehead to the crown of his head, and he was given a habit to wear like the other monks. Cuthbert was about 17 when he joined the community.

No trace remains of the monastery at Melrose where Cuthbert lived; the ruins that stand in the centre of the present town are of the twelfth-century Benedictine monastery. The site can still be seen, however, at Old Melrose, about two and a half miles from Melrose, in a large loop of the river. It is a beautiful place. A 19th-century writer described it in romantic terms.

A lovelier spot and one better fitted for prayerful meditation and the quiet growth of the religious spirit he could not have found. Sheltered from the winds of heaven and shut in from the intrusive foot of worldly men by the rocky scaur of Bemersyde, it is a monastery of Nature's own devising: embosomed in the rich green woods, almost encircled by the river Tweed, whose silver stream is here darkened by the depths of its pools and the shadow of the rock above, it is a temple in which the mind is raised from Nature up to Nature's God, is filled at once with restful peace and humble adoration. [5]

What kind of life did Cuthbert live in this beautiful place? The monastery at Old Melrose was still a new community when Cuthbert joined it around 651. Aidan had been its first abbot, having been given the site by King Oswald of Northumbria around 640, so the pattern of life was very much influenced by Iona and the Irish church. The buildings, scattered around the site, were of wood with rush-thatched roofs. The church would have been the largest building; smaller huts served as workshops and as living quarters for the monks.

Despite this peaceful setting, the monks did not live a life solely dedicated to prayer. Following the Irish example, they were enthusiastic missionaries, setting out, usually on foot, to preach the faith to those who had not yet heard it, and to encourage those already Christian. Cuthbert had great zeal for this work. Bede tells us:

He made a point of searching out those steep rugged places in the hills which other preachers dreaded to visit because of their poverty and squalor. This, to him, was a labour of love. He was so keen to preach that sometimes he would be away for a whole week or a fortnight, or even a month, living with the rough hill folk, preaching and calling them heavenwards by his example.[6]

About seven years after coming to Melrose, Cuthbert and some of the other monks moved south for a time to Ripon, in Yorkshire, where King Alhfrith had given Eata ground to build a monastery. Cuthbert was guestmaster of this new house, a responsible job and a sign of his ability. But the new community became entangled in the controversy (especially over the date of Easter) between those faithful to Roman customs and those still faithful to Irish practice, and the monastery was taken away from them and given to Wilfrid, a controversial figure, later bishop of York. The monks, Cuthbert among them, returned to Melrose. Around 660, after the death of Boisil, Cuthbert became prior. He was only 26.

Then came the move that would take Cuthbert to the place now associated with him more than any other—Lindisfarne. The monastery there had also been founded by Aidan, as a centre for the conversion of Northumbria. Eata, Cuthbert's abbot at Melrose, had been appointed as bishop of Lindisfarne around 664. According to some sources, when he moved he took Cuthbert with him to be prior of the monastery, but other evidence may point to a later date; it is not possible to be certain.

Whatever the date of his move, it wasn't an easy time for Cuthbert. The monks of Lindisfarne were set in their ways and reluctant to change. Cuthbert had to persevere and insist. Although he always did this kindly and gently, reading between the lines of Bede's account gives the impression of quite a battle, and of a considerable grasp of tactics by Cuthbert. He was patient and polite, but determined, and in the end the Lindisfarne monks were won round.

Perhaps it's not surprising that Cuthbert was also feeling an increasing call to a more solitary life, and Lindisfarne supplied the opportunity to explore this call. He was given permission to spend time on a tiny island, then known as Hobthrush Island but now called St Cuthbert's Isle, very near the monastery, just a few hundred metres from the shore. Like Lindisfarne itself, it was cut off by the tide twice a day. At these times, less than an acre of land remained above the high watermark. Today a plain wooden cross marks what may have been the site of Cuthbert's cell, and, sitting by it, one can look back to the site of Cuthbert's monastery. Perhaps this closeness to the monastery was the reason Cuthbert began to crave greater solitude. He moved to Inner Farne, one of the Farne Islands, which lie a few miles to the south-east of Lindisfarne. Now he had real solitude, with only the sea, the birds and the sea animals for company. The brothers would visit occasionally to bring supplies, but he tried as far as possible to be self-sufficient.

Even in such a remote place, however, Cuthbert was not able to be entirely alone. His reputation for holiness, and his miracles, drew people 'even from the remote parts of Britain',[7] but then came an even greater threat to his solitude. A new bishop of Lindisfarne was needed, and in 684 Cuthbert was elected. He was very reluctant to accept, and finally did so only when King Ecgfrith, Trumwine (who had been bishop of the Picts) and a number of other members of the synod sailed out to his island and wept and pleaded with him. He asked for, and was granted, a few more months on his island before being consecrated bishop at Easter 685.

Now he had to be constantly on the move. His diocese was very large, and he travelled widely, preaching, baptizing, confirming and giving advice. Although he spent less than two years as a bishop, there are many stories from that period which make clear the impact that he made. Cuthbert was now in his early 50s, however—a good age for anyone at that time—and he was suffering from his life of austerity and from a continuing weakness due to an illness he had experienced at Melrose.

In the end, the call of solitude was too strong. Cuthbert resigned as bishop immediately after Christmas 686 and returned to his hermitage. There he faced enormous and painful struggles with the forces of evil. His last days were dark and hard, but he remained faithful. When he knew he was dying, he asked to be buried on Inner Farne, and not returned to Lindisfarne. He knew that many people would want to visit his tomb, and he wished to spare the monks the distraction and problems of becoming a centre of pilgrimage. They ignored his advice. When he died on 20 March 687, they brought his body back to Lindisfarne and buried it in the monastery church. As we have already seen, Cuthbert's words came true: many pilgrims came to visit the church because of his presence there.

Cuthbert's life, outlined like this, is a compelling human story. Occasionally there are glimpses of how long ago and far away all these events were, although that can be forgotten in the vividness of the person who comes across in the biographies. Yet the seventh century was, in reality, immensely different from the 21st, and Cuthbert's story is more powerful and more comprehensible if we know a little of the background to his life. The shape of the British Isles was more or less the same as it is now, give or take the odd bit of coastline, but almost everything else was strange. If we could be transported back in time, we wouldn't be able to understand the language, enjoy the food, cope with the cold or the very basic living conditions, feel at home in the church, or make sense of who was in power and why. Knowing something of the differences in so many facets of life can help us to make sense of the very different religious presuppositions that we find just below the surface.

To begin with the broad picture, there was of course no such country as England, nor Scotland, Wales or Ireland. The British Isles were divided instead into a number of kingdoms, which were not necessarily stable or long-lived. Changing alliances and the fortunes of war were the background to a shifting picture of kingdoms, small or great, powerful or weak. In the seventh century there were at least twelve identifiable provinces whose rulers are regularly identified as kings, although most historians identify seven major kingdoms—Kent, Northumbria, Mercia, East Anglia, Sussex, Essex and Wessex. Cuthbert's life unfolded almost entirely within the kingdom of Northumbria, which stretched at its zenith from Yorkshire up almost to Edinburgh. It was one of the more stable and certainly one of the most powerful kingdoms, and was at its most extensive in the seventh century, Cuthbert's century. This stability, however, was relative.

Northumbria was formed through the amalgamation of the kingdoms of Bernicia, north of the Tyne, and Deira, between the Humber and the Tees. It was then enlarged through the conquest of older British kingdoms to the west and north. Unification came about in the reign of King Aethelfrith of Bernicia (c. 592–616). He was succeeded in both kingdoms by King Edwin of Deira (616–33), but for a time after Edwin's death, and again after the death of Oswald (634–42) who had also ruled a united kingdom, Bernicia and Deira were ruled separately. The last independent king of Deira was Oswine (644–51), and something of the instability and violence of the period can be seen by the fact that Oswine's reign ended when he was murdered by Oswy, king of Bernicia (642–70).

The shape of the church too was very different. The Romans had founded a few dioceses—we know of bishops of York and of the East Saxons (later of London) from their period—but very little of their organization survived. In the north and west, among the British, there were also some dioceses, probably corresponding to tribal divisions. In the fifth century, both Carlisle and Whithorn were the centres of dioceses, and the first bishop of Sodor and Man is recorded in 447. In the sixth century, there is evidence of dioceses around the Forth and in Fife, in Strathclyde, and in the valley of the Tweed. For the major part of these islands, however, Augustine's arrival in Canterbury and his consecration as the first bishop of a new diocese there was the beginning of a long process in the creation of a structure that could support the growing church. Rather like the kingdoms, the dioceses did not grow in an orderly manner: some were short-lived, others had periods with no bishop (or occasionally two). In 669, 70 years after Augustine's arrival, when Archbishop Theodore arrived in England to be Archbishop of Canterbury, he found only four dioceses with bishops—Northumbria, Rochester, Wessex and the diocese of the East Angles.

In the early years, the consecration of bishops often happened abroad, in Gaul or even in Rome, and such journeys were hazardous. Several prospective or newly consecrated bishops died on the way. It was some time before natives of these islands were sufficiently educated and experienced to take on this role. Ithamar, consecrated bishop of Rochester in 644, was the first Anglo-Saxon to occupy an English see.

Lindisfarne, with Aidan as its first bishop, was the diocese that covered most of Northumbria. Later in the century, from 664, there was also a diocese based in Hexham and, for a short period, a diocese for the Picts in the northern part of Northumbria, based at Abercorn on the Forth. The picture is complex, and much is uncertain. In addition, the dioceses, under the leadership of their bishops, were not necessarily the most powerful or most import-ant centres of Christianity. Influenced by the Celtic pattern, monasteries often took the lead as centres of worship and pastoral work, and in fact the bishops were often part of monastic com-munities. Bede, in his Life of Cuthbert, writes, 'Let no one be surprised to hear that Lindisfarne, as well as being an episcopal see… is also the home of an abbot and community, for indeed it is. The episcopal residence and the monastery are one and the same, and all the clergy are monks.'[8] This arrangement was not peculiar to Lindisfarne, and even those priests who were not monks were expected to live and work together, based in a minster church which had responsibility for pastoral care in the surrounding area.

Such care was very much needed. Faith was new and fragile, conversion often happened *en masse* in the wake of the conversion of the king, and in times of crisis there was a huge temptation to return to paganism—or not even to return, but to remain. The lasting conversion of the people of these islands took many years. By 664, nearly 70 years after the arrival of Augustine in Canterbury and Columba in Iona, Christianity was strongly rooted in Northumbria, East Anglia and Kent. Essex, however, which had been a Christian kingdom for a time, was lapsing back into paganism; Sussex and the Isle of Wight had not yet been visited by missionaries at all; and from the evidence of place names it seems likely that the present-day Surrey, Middlesex and Hertfordshire, as well as Wessex and the Midlands, were still deeply pagan. Bede, writing his *Ecclesiastical History of the English People* not long after Cuthbert's lifetime, still showed the influence of a deep-rooted belief in the supernatural and occult, and sought to prove that the Christian God was the match of any of the pagan deities.

If the large scale of politics and religion were very different, so too was life at the daily level of food and shelter. Stone buildings were very rare: churches were among the few examples, although the influence of Ireland meant that Northumbria's important churches were built in wood until late in the seventh century. Timber was also the main building material for secular buildings elsewhere, often with thatch for the roof. The average peasant house was a single all-purpose room, with an open hearth and a hole in the roof for the smoke, plus perhaps some outbuildings. Such houses, if not dispersed as individual farmsteads, were probably gathered in small hamlets or single-street villages; there appear to have been no towns as such at the start of the seventh century.

At the other end of the social scale from the peasants, kings or noblemen built fortified residences known as *burhs*. These consisted of a single-storey great hall, which served for meals, entertainment, daily business, and for the retainers to sleep in; plus smaller detached buildings called 'bowers', used as bedrooms by the owner, his family and guests, and also for kitchen, work-shops, and other domestic offices. The whole was surrounded by an earthwork and a stockade. Smaller landowners would have a less complex version of the *burh*, with a smaller main hall and fewer separate buildings. In all these buildings, floors were mostly of beaten earth or, above ground level, of suspended planking.

The range of food available to most people was limited: the mainstays of the average diet were cereals (especially barley), eaten as bread, beer (by far the most common drink) and pottage, which was a stew of cereals or pulses boiled with a limited range of vegetables to give flavour—leeks, onion, garlic, kale, turnip, carrot and parsnip. Bread was usually flat, baked on the hearth stones; only large establishments such as monasteries had ovens. Fruit was gathered from the wild, or cultivated: apples, pears, plums, cherries, blackberries, raspberries and strawberries are all known, as are nuts, mainly hazel.

The main source of protein was dairy produce: butter, cheese, curds and whey, buttermilk and eggs are all known from contemporary sources. Red meat was a regular part of the diet only for the upper classes; for others, pigs were the main source of meat, usually preserved as bacon or perhaps sausage, along with domestic fowls and perhaps some wild birds. Fish were caught but not farmed. Salt, as both a preservative and an essential part of the diet, was traded from earliest times and was one of the most substantial items of expenditure within a diet which was largely home-grown. Honey was used to sweeten: as the only source of concentrated sweetness, it must have been greatly prized. It was also made into mead, a luxury drink for the wealthy. Water was unsafe to drink, and although wine features often in literature, it too was a rarity in real life; it was imported for use in the Mass.

If the diet seems monotonous and lacking in interest to us,

so too would much of the visual side of life. Most clothing, for example, would have been either undyed or dyed with natural vegetable dyes, giving neutral, subdued colours. Cuthbert, we learn from Bede, 'wore quite ordinary clothes, neither remarkably neat nor noticeably slovenly. The monastery follows his example to this day. The monks are discouraged from wearing expensively dyed cloth and are expected to be content with natural wool.'[9] Both Anglo-Saxons and Celts, however, had a great love of colour, and luxury goods such as clothes for the rich and items for use in church often glittered and shimmered with rich colours and gemstones. From the colour words in Anglo-Saxon, we can get some sense of the range of colours possible—reds from pale brown through purple to scarlet; yellow from a dull, rather grey shade to the depth of saffron; blue dyed with woad; and words describing neutral colours (black, white, grey), some of which also mean 'shining'.

These words are in Anglo-Saxon, a language that developed from the variety of Germanic dialects brought by the various invaders— Angles, Saxons, Jutes—who came over from the northern mainland of Europe in the fifth century. Anglo-Saxon, in its turn, developed over the centuries into modern English. The native inhabitants of Britain spoke Celtic languages which are the ancestors of the later Welsh and Cornish languages. Latin was the language of worship and of the administration of the church, and was therefore taught in the monastic schools. When Bede became a monk, he had to learn Latin: it was not a living spoken language in Northumbria.

Because Latin was the language of scholarship, while English was the everyday spoken language, most written records are in Latin. Apart from one fragment of a poem, there is nothing written in English from the time of Cuthbert apart from some laws (the first written in English) and glosses (English translations or explanations) on some Latin texts, written between the lines of the manuscript, but we know that much poetry did exist, and was handed down by word of mouth.

Books were rare and expensive, written by hand. They were

among the main items brought back by those who travelled abroad, especially from France, Spain and Italy. Libraries remained small and limited compared to those that had existed in the ancient world. Alexandria in Egypt had perhaps 600,000 volumes; Cassiodorus, writing in sixth-century Italy, had 2000–3000. Bede, who was the most widely read man of his day, is known to have used 175 titles, and the library in his monastery of Jarrow was perhaps two to three times that size. Lindisfarne at the time of Cuthbert would have had considerably fewer volumes.

How many people would have been able to make use of such libraries? It is hard to say, as the terms 'literate' and 'illiterate' were used in a rather different way from how we now understand them. 'Literate' was used only of clergy who could both read and write in Latin. 'Illiterate' could mean either a layman or a cleric who could not read and write in Latin. So the category of 'literate' does not include clergy who could read but not write Latin (and these were separable skills), or who could read English; or lay people who could read or write either language. Reading aloud was one of the particular skills taught to novice monks, and was not easy to master, involving as it did 'reading aloud in a foreign language, often no doubt by the poor light of the candle, from a book which had been written by hand and which might well have had no punctuation'.[10]

This may perhaps be a good image of the difficulty for today's reader of making sense of the life of a saint of the seventh century: much is foreign, hard to make out; the light flickers, sometimes illuminating beautifully, sometimes leaving us very much in the dark. It is easy to misunderstand, to read back into the story our assumptions—assumptions so much part of our mindset that we don't even know we have them. Remembering how different life was can be one way of noticing at least some of our assumptions and perhaps learning to set them aside.

Despite the distance and the differences, however, Cuthbert continues to influence people today. How does this happen? It's quite easy to understand how he became and remained famous in his lifetime. Even for a time afterwards, there would have been many people who had met him and therefore remembered him and were influenced by his life and example, or, as time went on, who met someone who had known him. What about centuries later, though, when everyone who'd encountered him in life was long since dead? Well, one of the things about saints is that they demonstrate vividly that death isn't the end. If we believe in the resurrection of Christ—and that in his resurrection he was the forerunner of life beyond death, life through death, for all who believe—then the saints, who are prime exemplars of faith, should above all be still alive, still working in this world, as Christ is.

My own encounter with Cuthbert was, I believe, a vivid example of this. I knew about him; I had visited Lindisfarne, and had been to his shrine in Durham Cathedral, still a place of pilgrimage, though now simple and undecorated—just a slab with his name on it, in a small chapel behind the high altar. I knew about him, but I hadn't met him. One summer I was with a meditation group of which I had long been a member. We were spending a week in Northumberland, enjoying the chance to spend more time together and at our practice than we could spend in the usual evening meeting. Part of our plan was to visit holy places and meditate there. We'd been to Lindisfarne; now, on a wet, grey, chilly August day, we were in Durham. While the leaders met to plan the day, I offered to take other group members into the cathedral and help them get their bearings.

As I stood at the west end of the great Romanesque building, pointing out the Galilee Chapel behind us, burial place of the Venerable Bede (Cuthbert's biographer), and indicating that Cuthbert's shrine was at the far, eastern end, I felt Cuthbert drawing me to him. Sudden and totally unexpected, it was unmistakably him, drawing me to his shrine with a visceral pull, impossible to resist. Leaving my charges, I sped up the central aisle, through the crowds of visitors, left at the choir screen, down the side aisle, and up the short flight of steps to the shrine. I sank to my knees, half crying, half laughing, 'I'm here, I'm here!'

Cuthbert had reached out from the unimaginable past and made it very clear that he wasn't confined to it. It was like nothing so much as falling in love, and, like falling in love, nothing has been quite the same since.

✻ ✻ ✻

HERE AND NOW

The title of this chapter comes from the prologue to the Life of Cuthbert written by an anonymous monk of Lindisfarne. He writes to Bishop Eadfrith, who had asked him to write the book, 'So with great joy I undertook your loving command. For this record of St Cuthbert is of great gain and value to myself. Indeed it is in itself a ready path to virtue to know what he was.'[11] This monk may well have known Cuthbert himself, and certainly knew those who had lived with him. He wrote his book only 13 years or so after Cuthbert's death, but how can we who live more than 1300 years later find joy, value, and a 'ready path to virtue' in knowing about Cuthbert?

At the end of each chapter, I want to make some suggestions as to how we might indeed do this. It will require some imagination, some patience, some willingness to think differently perhaps, but the potential rewards are great.

For this chapter, the task is to consider how we connect with our history, with our tradition, in ways that are life-giving and life-changing. We are heirs to so much, and are impoverished if we look only at today's scene, today's story. To begin with, you might like to recall some figures from your own history of faith who have been important. Start perhaps with someone whom you actually knew, and gradually work back into history. Spend some time recalling why these people were important, how knowing them or knowing of them helped you, and what their gifts to you have been. Remember and give thanks for any times when you have experienced the centuries dissolving and a figure from the past becoming real and alive for you.

See yourself now as part of a long line of Christians, stretching back to the time of Christ himself. Give thanks for those who have passed on the faith through the centuries, so that you might come to faith now. Plant yourself firmly in the good soil of your tradition, nourished by it and enabled to grow by it.

CHAPTER 2

TO DESIRE GOD MORE

Like anyone newly in love, I wanted to know everything about this person who had suddenly become vivid and alive to me. Bede's Life in prose was easy to find; I devoured it. The anonymous Life was harder to track down, but I did that too, and read it rapidly. As I read, I became gradually more perplexed. These so-called biographies weren't telling me what I really wanted to know. There was little about what Cuthbert looked like, what he said, his struggles or his inner life; instead there was a succession of miracles and other stories whose main elements and patterns I recognized from the Bible. Often, indeed, the writer himself points out the parallel.

Cuthbert is provided with food while on a journey, just as Elijah had been.[1] He heals the wife of a sheriff called Hildmer who is possessed by a demon, and does so from a distance.[2] Abbess Aefflaed and one of her nuns are cured by a linen cincture, or sash, sent by Cuthbert, as the early Christians in the book of Acts had been by handkerchiefs touched by Paul (Acts 19:11–12).[3] He blesses water and sends it to be sprinkled over a desperately ill woman, who is immediately healed, and, like Peter's mother-in-law (Luke 4:39), 'ministered to those who had ministered to her, the patient tending the physicians'.[4] Merely by tasting water, he makes it taste like wine, and excellent wine at that, like Jesus at the wedding in Cana (John 2:1–11).[5]

Perhaps others could see what I could not in these works? I began to read more widely, looking at what other people had written about Cuthbert. Far from helping, this made things worse. I discovered that even some of what had sounded original in the biographies was, in fact, taken from the Lives of other saints. Parts of the first two chapters of the anonymous Life, for example, were taken word for word from biographies of Antony of Egypt and Martin of Tours, and the prologue is largely a conventional preface, found in these Lives and also in others after Cuthbert's. There is another exact extract from the Life of Martin later in the anonymous Life, in chapter 4, and a number of strong similarities between the ministry styles of Martin and Cuthbert, some of the miracles being claimed for both of them.

A few months after beginning my quest, I had to face an uncomfortable truth: these were not biographies at all. They were hagiographies—Lives of a saint—and that was a very different kind of writing. Was it possible to know anything from them about Cuthbert as a distinct, unique individual, or was he effectively hidden for ever behind the conventions of this form of writing? It felt like hoping to recognize someone in the street from seeing only an icon of them.

This was a low point in my search for Cuthbert, but having once recognized the difficulties and accepted the need to read the sources in a different way than I'd expected, the darkness and fog began to lift a little. As I circled around the questions, occasional shafts of light illuminated a real person, in the same way as the icon, though not a conventional portrait, does show something deeply real about the person portrayed.

A hagiography, I learned:

...is above all pragmatic, practical: it shows one of that great cloud of witnesses in the detail of his life on earth as he walked in the footsteps of the Man of Galilee; and it poses the invitation of the angels at the tomb: 'Come and see; he is not here, he is risen.' The accounts of Cuthbert are not only a window onto the dead past; they are a stream of living water where he who is alive in Christ shows the race that is set before those

who come after. They are not rather poor biographies; they are first-rate hagiographies.[6]

Here was an important clue: the reason why much of what I had hoped to find was missing was not because Bede or the anonymous monk were bad writers but because their concerns were very different from those of most writers and readers today. They wanted to show Cuthbert as an example of holiness, and to record how God had recognized his holiness and dedication by working signs and wonders through Cuthbert, both in his life and after his death. It was natural, therefore, for them to use the stories from scripture which were at the heart of their own faith as templates for the stories of Cuthbert. They did also wish, however, to make it clear that what they wrote was trustworthy, so they often noted who had told them a particular story, or who had been an eyewitness of the event, and sometimes even what that person was now doing. One of those who drank the water that tasted of wine, for example, became a monk in the same monastery as Bede, and told him the story.

It is likely that Bede mentioned only some of the eyewitnesses whose testimonies he used. In the prologue to his book, he speaks of writing nothing 'that has not been obtained by rigorous examination of trustworthy witnesses', and tells how he investigated the whole of Cuthbert's life 'with the help of those who had actually known him. I occasionally mention some of their names in the body of the book so that you can see for yourselves exactly what the sources are.'[7] The anonymous Lindisfarne monk also quotes a number of eyewitnesses, often different from those in Bede's Life; and sometimes he cites an eyewitness where Bede does not, though Bede must have had the anonymous Life as one of the sources for his work.

Even here, though, where we seem to be stepping on to more solid ground, all is not what it seems. I learnt that in hagiographies 'the appeal to witnesses... helps to give the impression of veracity, though... this method of vouching for the truth of a story was in the regular tradition and did not necessarily mean much.'[8] Colgrave points out that the quoting of apparently eyewitness accounts goes back to one of the very early examples of saints' Lives, Athanasius' Life of Antony. Athanasius claims that he is writing only what he has learned on the authority of Antony himself. 'But many of the stories which follow of fights with devils, of visions, and miracles of healing are to say the least of a highly imaginative order.'[9] This does not mean that the authors are lying, or that we can learn nothing from what they write, but it means that we need to be clear what kind of truth they were writing. To do that, we have to enter the world of the hagiography, and learn to think as their writers and readers did.

Hagiography was the main literary form for several hundred years, from around AD400 to 800. The Lives of the saints provided a large pool of suitable reading for monks, who were a considerable proportion of those able to read at all. How did these books come to be written? There were, after all, no publishers to commission a Life of the latest saintly celebrity. In fact, most hagiographies were not written all at once, but developed in stages, in response to liturgical need. A local saint died (and saints were not canonized centrally, but recognized locally), so the priest held a mass each year on the anniversary of the death. In order to have something to read which was particular to the saint, he gathered local memories and wrote a brief biography. This was noted on the calendar so that it could be used again next year. If the saint became famous beyond the locality, and pilgrims began to visit, one mass was no longer enough, and an office of the saint began to develop, making more readings necessary.

Eventually the readings may have been gathered together into an entire Life. In a society with few written records and generally short lifespans, actual details of the saint's life might have been scanty, so the written Life was filled out with stories from the tradition, which described the expected characteristics of a saint and recounted typical miracles.

So hagiography, like scripture, is not primarily history, but theology. Yet, like the scripture, it is located in history. As it is important, when reading scripture, to know whether a particular book or passage is, for example, poetry, wisdom literature or history, and to read it through that lens, so with hagiography. Bede, for example, does not usually cite eyewitnesses to material historical truth, but to miracles. He is citing them to back up the claims of his story to *ethical* truth—that is, to assert that God was truly working through Cuthbert.

In this way, hagiographies are a form of writing which assert that the God who worked in scripture is still working. The Gospels are not just a story of the past, to be looked back on with wonder, but are alive and effective now. The Christ who called the apostles and sent them out to preach the word is still calling, even in the farthest parts of the world, and still sending out men and women to do his work. Those who were called were part of a living tradition, drawing for their inspiration not only on the scriptures, but also on the saints who had gone before them, known through the hagiographies that recorded their lives. Seen in this light, these apparently remote and often frankly peculiar stories can aid our attempts to let the Gospels be alive and effective in our lives. Bede, in the Prologue to his Life of Cuthbert, addressed to the Lindisfarne monks, gives a clear description of his purpose in writing the book: 'When, in reading my book,' he writes, 'your hearts are raised to a more burning desire for the Kingdom of Heaven'.[10] Such books had a clear spiritual purpose.

The classic Lives that set the pattern for most of the hagiographies of our period were those of Antony, the Egyptian hermit traditionally seen as the father of the monastic life; Benedict, Italian writer of the rule that shaped Western monasticism for many centuries; and Martin, French monk and bishop. They tend to follow a standardized form, starting with a brief account of the saint's birth, along with any prophecies at the time or in his early life. Then there is a series of miracles associated with his life and ministry, followed by an account of his death, and finally the miracles that took place at his tomb. Usually included also are a list of his virtues, some accounts of struggles with devils and temptations, a model sermon and, on the deathbed, a farewell oration. You may be able to see how at least some of this follows the pattern of the Gospels themselves.

We have already seen how some of what, at first sight, seems individual in the Lives of Cuthbert is in fact taken from one or other of these earlier Lives. Given the various facets of Cuthbert's life as monk, hermit and bishop, perhaps this is not surprising— and the process continued. Lives written after those of Cuthbert in their turn borrow from them. For example, Eddius, who wrote the Life of St Wilfrid specifically in response to the anonymous Life of Cuthbert, lifted entire passages from it in his attempt to support his claims for the sanctity of his hero. Felix copied his account of the discovery of St Guthlac's incorrupt body exactly from Bede's description of the same event in Cuthbert's life, 'written by the most widely circulated author of the day about the most renowned saint in Britain'.[11]

The writers of hagiographies were not, therefore, trying to be original, and what would now seem blatant plagiarism would not have been seen as such then. They were asking different questions from those asked by a modern biographer. Cuthbert's hagiographers were working under constraints that would make most biographers give up in despair. Cuthbert left nothing written—no letters, sermons or prayers from which to glean an idea of his mind, heart and spirit—and it seems almost certain that neither the monk of Lindisfarne who wrote the anonymous Life nor Bede ever met Cuthbert. In addition, there were complex questions of church politics, especially the different emphases and practices of Roman-influenced and Irish-influenced Christianity which, as we shall see later, influenced what could be written. But the question that shaped these works was one that could still be answered despite all these apparent disadvantages.

Benedicta Ward writes of the hagiographers of Cuthbert:

The question these men asked about Cuthbert may not be ours, but it is a valid one; they were not interested in his noble connections, his love of gold, beer, or small animals, not even in whether he was clever, brave, or great; they only wanted to know how this frail human being had put on the Lord Jesus Christ through life and into death.[12]

In order to do this, she goes on to say, the writers present real events (and that is important), not primarily for the sake of those events themselves, but in such a way that the significance of these events in relation to God and to God's work in the life of the saint is brought out.

It might seem that this style of writing would be guaranteed to remove any possibility of real connection with the saint but, by some paradox, it does not.

In accounts of saints' lives, the common opinion about events and people was constantly shot through with the inner meaning of Christian sanctity. It is very interesting that this allusive, sideways, oblique way of writing about people in fact brings them more vividly alive than any other way. The first-generation Christians in England, Hilda, Chad, Wilfrid, Aidan, Etheldreda and Cuthbert, were written about as saints, but this was not to make them seem formal bloodless characters; on the contrary, these Lives present pictures of them that print them on the mind's eye with vigour and vitality... Perhaps it was not after all so strange that to see someone in their own chosen light, which was that of Christ, should make not for distance but for all the warmth and closeness of real holiness.[13]

Author Thomas Head says that saints were as real for those who read about them, heard about them, prayed to them and went on pilgrimage to their shrines as characters from television soap operas are today. Perhaps the hagiography could be seen as in some ways parallel to the celebrity interview in *OK* or *Hello* magazines, which also have their conventions and their standard form. The famous are seen and written about in the light of their fame, the saints in the light of their sanctity. Today's cult of celebrity has borrowed from that of saints; there may even some-times be a belief that fame confers power, seen in the practice of footballers or pop stars visiting sick children, and the huge prices paid at times for anything that they have owned—modern-day relics.

The hagiographers are perhaps more realistic, however. Although they do describe the saints as people with power—power to heal, raise the dead, defeat enemies, calm wild beasts—they are always clear that this power comes from God. Holiness brings access to God's power, which the saints use on behalf of others and for their good.

As we have seen, it helps in reading hagiographies to use some of the same tools as in reading scripture, but the connections are even closer than that. Scripture itself is quoted extensively in hagiographies, both directly and through allusions and turns of phrase. It is tempting to take these quotations as mere trimmings, and skip over them to get to the stories of the saint, but in fact they are a crucial part of the writers' armoury, and can tell us much about the saint who is the subject of the hagiography.

It was common at this time to read the scriptures on different levels, and both Bede and the anonymous author would have been familiar with the ways in which the fathers of the Church inter-preted many key passages of the Bible. Douglas Dales lists the four levels of understanding: 'the actual history; its moral meaning; its bearing upon the life of the church in its sacraments and spiritual life; and its eternal meaning as a window into the kingdom of heaven'.[14] These often subtle and sophisticated understandings became, through scriptural quotations and allusions in the hagio-graphies, as it were a lens through which to see the life of the saint. Perhaps sometimes the lens distorts, but at other times it helps us to see more clearly. The saints themselves were, after all, shaped and influenced by the same way of reading the scripture. It is not an alien imposition, though it may seem so to us, with our very different ways of studying and understanding the Bible.

It need not lead to a monochrome interpretation of events, either. Benedicta Ward gives a fascinating account of the different scriptural lenses placed by the anonymous monk and Bede over their accounts of the same event in the life of Cuthbert—his visit, as a monk of Melrose, to the abbey of Coldingham. Aebbe, the abbess, features in other stories of Cuthbert, and was the sister of King Oswy.

The story in both sources is very similar. Cuthbert, invited by Aebbe to visit the community, which consisted of both monks and nuns, stayed for several days, teaching and preaching by word and by example. It was his custom to rise during the night, and he did so while at Coldingham, going down to the beach to pray and sing. He waded out into the sea and continued his prayers there. One night one of the monks followed him, curious to find out where he was going and what he was doing. He saw Cuthbert praying on the beach and then in the water. When the saint came out of the sea, he knelt down on the beach and continued in prayer, and two creatures (Bede says otters, the anonymous monk calls them 'little sea animals') came out of the sea with him, and dried his feet with their fur, warming them with their breath. Cuthbert blessed them, and they returned to the sea. Cuthbert returned to the abbey and joined the nuns and monks in their morning office. The brother who had spied on Cuthbert was terrified by what he had seen, and confessed with great fear to the saint. Cuthbert forgave him, on condition that he told no one what he had seen.

It seems an attractive story.

A walk on the beach at night, so often fruitful for the English. A man alone by the sea, singing to himself and taking a dip, with small furry animals rubbing round his ankles. How attractive; is this perhaps, and

how consoling it would be, the spirituality of Cuthbert? But this most
private, intimate moment of the prayer of Cuthbert is not so superficial
for either the anonymous writer or Bede when they place over it the lens
of the Scriptures.[15]

The anonymous writer sees Cuthbert as Daniel. Coldingham had
a reputation for laxity, and perhaps the life of this double monastery was not as well regulated as it should have been. Feasting,
drinking and gossip took the place of prayer and study, and the
nuns spent their time weaving elaborate clothing for themselves.
So Cuthbert is thrown into this 'den' as Daniel was into the den of
lions, and the animals minister to them both. Another layer of
meaning comes with the knowledge that the fathers of the Church
saw Daniel as a forerunner of Christ, who became a slave as Daniel
did, and came down into this world as into a den of wild animals.

Bede, on the other hand, sees the story through the lens of the
transfiguration, quoting the words of Jesus to his disciples after
they had seen him in his glory: 'Tell no one about the vision until
after the Son of Man has been raised from the dead' (Matthew
17:9). For Bede, as for the Fathers of the Church, the transfiguration was the second epiphany of Christ, the first being his
baptism in the Jordan. In both, Christ was revealed as the Son of
God, once by water and once by light. Hence the terror of the
monk watching Cuthbert at prayer: he saw in him the face of
Christ, the new Adam, at peace with the animals and restored to
right relationship with them. The Coldingham monk becomes in a
sense the third otter: he too is prostrate at the feet of Cuthbert
and, through his tears of repentance, is brought into the new
relationship of creation with its creator, of the Christian with his
transfigured Lord.

This example gives us a glimpse of the richness inherent in the
interweaving of hagiography and scripture, and sheds light, I hope,
on a different way of reading, but one which is crucial to grasp if
we hope to enter the world of the writers and readers of the Lives

of the saints. Understanding the tradition within which they were written helps us to move beyond the conventional forms and to see the real people behind them. Douglas Dales has a useful image.

Hagiography conformed during this period to certain patterns... it reflected a corporate spiritual expectation and perception. Yet within this corpus of literature, no hagiography simply mimics another. There is much incidental historical detail embedded within it, and it is possible to discern the lineaments of individual personalities. But hagiographies are not biographies: they are more like icons—true images rooted in history, but seen in the perspective of the eternal purpose of God in Christ. [16]

So what of the true image of Cuthbert can we find in the Lives? As icons have a family resemblance, but each saint has his or her own attributes, so there are individual touches in the Lives of Cuthbert which help us to see him through the form and tradition.

The passages that are largely taken from earlier hagiographies, and which therefore seem to have little to give us about the saint, can paradoxically also be a source of individual information about our saint. If an author has deliberately changed one or two things in an otherwise identical passage, it seems likely that this has been done for a reason and reflects something of the individuality of the saint. So the anonymous monk of Lindisfarne, writing about Cuthbert's life on Inner Farne, takes a description almost word for word from Athanasius' Life of Antony, an obvious source for one writing about a solitary life. But where Antony is described as a man who 'never through the excess of hilarity broke into laughter', Cuthbert is 'at all hours... happy and joyful'. [17]

Having more than one source is also helpful as we compare stories from the different hagiographies, seeing which are common, which are peculiar to one version, and how stories develop over the years from the earliest Life, by the anonymous monk of Lindisfarne, to the latest, the brief account in Bede's *Ecclesiastical History.*

Bede changed some of what he himself wrote. For example, in his account of Cuthbert's time at Ripon, in the prose Life he gives no reason for the expulsion of the Melrose monks but simply says, 'All the ways of this world are as fickle and unstable as a sudden storm at sea. Eata and Cuthbert and all the rest were thrown out of Ripon and the monastery they had built given over to other monks.'[18] In the *Ecclesiastical History*, however, he speaks of the reasons (though indirectly), giving us information for which, though we might have guessed it, this is the only actual evidence. Bede says that Ahlfrith, the sub-king of Deira under his father, Oswy, 'rightly preferred [the] teaching [of Wilfrid] to all the traditions of the Irish and had therefore given him a monastery of forty hides in the place called Ripon. He had presented the site, a short time before, to those who followed Irish ways; but because when given the choice they preferred to renounce the site rather than change their customs, he gave it to one who was worthy of the place both by his doctrine and his way of life.'[19] Although Bede does not here mention Cuthbert, we know from his prose Life that Cuthbert was one of those expelled, and therefore know that Cuthbert followed the Irish tradition of calculating the date of Easter, a source of much controversy at the time.

Being aware of the earlier hagiographies that the authors quote is also helpful, as we see that they do not generally follow in its entirety any of the earlier Lives, but choose particular elements from specific Lives. This would seem to show that they had some real knowledge of the saint about whom they were writing, and were shaping their use of the material to reveal him.

In a further paradox, the very fact that there are common stories and themes can tell us something: they demonstrate that Cuthbert was living consciously within a tradition, and would therefore shape his life, actions and prayer by that tradition. A knowledge of the tradition, therefore, will in itself give us insight into the life of the individual within it. Bonner gives a striking illustration of this principle, writing of the parallels between the life of Cuthbert and the life of Seraphim of Sarov, a Russian saint born in 1759. Like Cuthbert, he became a monk, and spent some years as a hermit before duty called him back to the monastery, where he became a much sought-after spiritual guide. Even the accounts of their deaths have many points of similarity. Eleven centuries separate the two saints, and neither Seraphim nor those who wrote about him can have had any knowledge of Cuthbert, but they both drew on the same Egyptian ascetic monastic tradition exemplified especially in the life of Antony. Bonner continues:

Accordingly, when we find details in the life of Cuthbert which seem to draw upon the life of Antony, we should not too readily conclude that Bede or the Lindisfarne author have borrowed from the one to make a traditional and acceptable setting for the other. We may, or may not, accept the possibility that either Antony or Cuthbert actually fought with demons; it is not necessary to assume that Cuthbert is said to have done so simply because this was said of Antony.[20]

The Lives, then, can tell us more than we might first think. Another source of information is the few physical relics of Cuthbert. When his coffin was opened in 1899 and the bones examined, it was recorded that he was strongly built and 5'8" to 5'9" tall—taller than average for a man of those days. The objects buried with him indicate what was thought to be important to him or very much identified with him. Most of the cloth that has survived, though ancient, was probably part of later gifts to the shrine of the saint rather than original, but there are three things that seem likely to have actually belonged to Cuthbert—a pectoral cross, a portable altar and a comb. They can still be seen today in the Treasury at Durham Cathedral.

The pectoral cross, worn by a bishop, was hung round Cuthbert's neck on a silk cord with a gold twist. It is small, only about 2.5 inches across, but very beautiful, made of gold and garnet, with a shell collar surrounding a central garnet. The shell is not native to Britain, coming perhaps from the Mediterranean or even the Indian Ocean. The cross was almost certainly made in Northumbria during the seventh century, and perhaps it is not too fanciful to imagine it as being made especially for Cuthbert on his consecration as bishop. It speaks to me of Cuthbert's dignity as a bishop, of office accepted reluctantly but lived out faithfully to the end.

The portable altar has been encased in silver, perhaps in the ninth century, but in its original simple form—a small oak slab, only 5.25 by 4.75 inches, decorated with five crosses and a Latin inscription *in honorem S Petrus* ('in honour of St Peter')—is of the seventh century. It speaks to me of Cuthbert's willingness to go where people needed him, to bring Christ to the fringe places of his world.

The comb is made of bone, with teeth on two sides and a large hole in the middle. It resembles some Coptic combs of the period and may have come from Egypt. It is plain and undecorated, and it seems unlikely that it would have been placed in the coffin unless it had belonged to Cuthbert. It speaks to me of simplicity and of basic human needs: even saints need to comb their hair.

These small glimpses of the physical Cuthbert, together with a careful reading of the hagiographies, studying the common elements from the tradition, the changes that speak of the individual, and the light shed by the scriptures, all contribute finally to a real picture of a real person. My search had been longer and more complex than I'd expected, but I had been rewarded with more than just a typical saint. It may be true that 'the real Cuthbert is hard to find and far to seek'[21] but the journey repays the effort. As an icon repays many hours spent gazing in prayer, learning to look through it to the God who inspired it, so the Lives of Cuthbert repay slow, careful and prayerful reading, using both the resources of scholarship and the eyes of faith.

* * *

HERE AND NOW

The questions with which I had to grapple in order to find Cuthbert in the hagiographies have much wider applications. How do we 'read' any document, any evidence, from the past, in ways that honour its context but also bring it alive now?

Of course, this question applies especially to the Bible. We are always faced with a juggling act between becoming so interested in the context that we avoid the challenge of the writings to our own lives, and going straight to the question 'What does this say to me?' while ignoring the thought patterns of the time in which it was written and the questions the author was trying to answer then. It's important to know which extreme tempts us more, and to try to redress the balance consciously as we read, study and pray with the scriptures. If you know you can get stuck in the context, make a commitment to look for how the story or teaching can shed light on your own life. As the hagiographers place the scriptural stories over the life of Cuthbert, look for the connections and the places where a scriptural story, image or allusion can be seen in your story. If your temptation is to ignore the context altogether, make a commitment to some serious study, perhaps of a favourite book or character, looking for the connections to the tradition and for the light shed on the text by a knowledge of why, when and for whom it was written down.

Another exercise that may relate to the themes of this chapter is to consider who your heroes and role models are. Are you conscious of shaping your life with God in the light of an earlier Christian individual, group or tradition? From whom do you take your values? In a world where 'heroes' are often those who excel at sport or at making large sums of money, it is easy to be swept along. Time spent consciously choosing whom you want to emulate is a valuable part of the spiritual life.

Is there a particular saint whom you think of as a 'soul friend'? This is something worth cultivating. Like all relationships, it will take time and effort, but they are repaid by the knowledge of having a friend who has walked the path of the gospel before you, with the sense of closeness and support that gives, and by nourishing a particular link into the tradition. Such a saint can become an icon, whether literally or metaphorically, who draws you closer to the God who created and called you both.

CHAPTER 3

'FAITH WORKING THROUGH LOVE'

Towards the end of Cuthbert's life, Tunbert, bishop of Hexham, was deposed, perhaps because of an argument with the king. Although originally the monastery of Iona had appointed bishops of Northumbria, by this time it was the kings who held this power.

A new bishop was needed, so a great synod was held in Northumbria, near the river Aln, probably somewhere around the village now called Alnmouth. Archbishop Theodore presided over the meeting, and the king, Ecgfrith, was present. Unanimously they elected Cuthbert as bishop. Letters and messengers were sent to him at his hermitage on Farne, but he was reluctant to leave the solitary life and refused to come. Finally a delegation was sent, including the king himself and Trumwine, who had been bishop of the Picts but was now retired and living at the monastery at Whitby. They were joined by many of the brothers from Lindisfarne, and they begged Cuthbert to consent to be bishop. Finally he agreed, but not happily, and 'was led away unwillingly and under compulsion, weeping and wailing'.[1] Cuthbert was consecrated in York, on Easter Day 685, to the diocese of Lindisfarne. He had asked if he might stay in that diocese rather than moving to Hexham, so Eata, then bishop of Lindisfarne, had resigned and moved to Hexham instead.

Although it is traditional in hagiographies that the saints accept high office reluctantly, I am sure that this story does reflect some reality. Cuthbert had waited a long time to enter the solitary life, which he saw as more perfectly following God, and would undoubtedly have been reluctant to leave it for the busy life of a bishop, engaged with powerful people and with the politics of the day. Often in Cuthbert's life there were forces pulling him in apparently incompatible directions—life in community, prayer in solitude, and leadership in the church.

Choosing to respond to the call of the church upon him to be a bishop was one of the last choices made by Cuthbert in a life marked by them. The first was dramatic—his choice of the monastic life. As we have already seen, he made this choice in response to a dramatic vision, which he believed to be of the soul of Aidan (himself a monk and a bishop of Lindisfarne) ascending to heaven on the night of his death. Boisil, who welcomed Cuthbert to the monastery at Melrose, later prophesied that he would become a bishop. This happened in the last week of Boisil's life. Knowing that he was dying, he chose to spend his last week studying with Cuthbert the Gospel of John. He had a commentary in seven sections, and they used one each day. Although John's Gospel has enough in it to fuel a lifetime's study, they were able to finish it in the week they had available, because they 'dealt not with the profound arguments but with the simple things of "the faith which worketh by love"'.[2]

Cuthbert rarely spoke of this prophecy except occasionally to lament to his brothers his belief that, even if he were to live an entirely solitary life on an island cut off from the world, he would not be free from the cares of the world. He acknowledged, though, that it might be God's will that he hold high office. In a conversation with Aelfflaed, sister of Ecgfrith and abbess of Whitby, she wondered at his preference for a barren rock in the middle of the ocean over the high honour and dignity of being a bishop. '"I know I am not worthy," he replied, "but I know that the decree of the Supreme Ruler cannot be escaped, no matter where one might flee to."'[3] In his election as bishop, his fears were fulfilled and the prophecy of Boisil, given so many years before, had come true.

Cuthbert's personal struggle with the choices required of him was echoed in the church in his century. It is perhaps easy to look back and think that we see a simpler, less complicated time, when the church was united and many of today's controversies had not arisen, but human nature being what it is, and the church being made up from the beginning of fallible human beings, that golden age does not exist except in our dreams. In Cuthbert's time the church was, as now, subject to division and difficulty, to personality clashes and disagreements. As we have seen, one of the most marked was over the way of calculating the date of Easter. It sounds a simple, practical issue, but it generated much controversy because of what it symbolized about the church, and about authority in the church.

Bede is vehement in his writing about the necessity of holding to the right (which was, for him, the Roman) way of calculating the date. He sees Aidan as in many ways the perfect bishop, one who 'cultivated peace and love, purity and humility; he was above anger and greed, and despised pride and conceit; he set himself to keep and to teach the laws of God, and was diligent in study and prayer'[4] but feels that he must add, 'One cannot commend or approve his inadequate knowledge of the proper observance of Easter.'[5]

The problem was that Aidan came from the Celtic, Irish tradition, and had been trained on Iona, a monastery founded from Ireland. Although Ireland itself had been evangelized from Rome, Irish Christians had developed a very distinctive style of church and monastic life. Part of this was a different way of calculating Easter, which often led to their celebrating the feast on a different day. This was not a problem as long as the two churches were separated by distance, but in Britain at this time the two came together, the Roman influence spreading northwards from Canterbury, and the Irish southwards from Iona. Cuthbert's time and place were precisely where they met, so he was necessarily affected by the tensions caused by those who, in good conscience, held different views.

The question was supposed to have been settled at the Council of Nicea in 325. The early Christians had celebrated Easter on the Jewish Passover, which fell on the 14th day of the first month of the Jewish year, the month of Nisan, but it came to be felt that Easter should be celebrated on a Sunday, and that keeping it on the Jewish feast should be avoided. The Council of Nicea tried to legislate for this by condemning as heretics those who kept Easter on Nisan 14 and stipulating that Easter should always be celebrated on a Sunday, but they did not make clear whether it was acceptable to keep Easter on Nisan 14 should that day be a Sunday. The Roman church thought not, and therefore kept Easter on the Sunday between Nisan 15 and 21; the Irish church chose the Sunday between Nisan 14 and 20. A further complication was introduced by the existence of various calendars used to calculate these dates. By the seventh century there were three in use—one Alexandrian, one French, and one Irish.

Although all this detail can seem confusing and irrelevant, it helped me to understand how people of good will could in good conscience find themselves on different sides. Each valued the tradition; each believed that in their practice they were following it.

The Easter problem came to a head in Northumbria in a very personal way, within a marriage, though a royal one. King Oswy of Northumbria married Eanfled, daughter of Edwin, who, though born in Northumbria, had been brought up in Kent. She therefore kept the Roman Easter, while Oswy kept the Irish one. This meant that Oswy could be keeping Easter with feasting and revelry while his queen and her court were entering into Holy Week and a time of fasting and penitence. The Synod of Whitby in 664 was an attempt to come to a common mind. Bede gives a vivid description of the meeting, which ended with Oswy giving judgment for the Roman side, led by Wilfrid, a controversial and combative character who would himself in the future fall foul of disagreements with King Ecgfrith. The Irish side was led by Colman, bishop of Lindisfarne.

There is no mention of Cuthbert himself being at Whitby, but he was certainly affected by the controversy. As we have seen, he was one of the monks from Melrose who went in the late 650s to make a new foundation at Ripon, on land given by Oswy's son Alhfrith. But Alhfrith had been a pupil of Wilfrid and, when the Melrose monks refused to change their customs on tonsure and the date of Easter to conform to the Roman practice, he took the land away from them and gave it to Wilfrid. Cuthbert had first-hand experience, therefore, of how these disagreements could have practical effects on real lives. It was also indirectly due to the Synod that he came to Lindisfarne as prior. When Colman, unable to accept the outcome of the Synod of Whitby, resigned as bishop of Lindisfarne and returned to Scotland, he was replaced as bishop by Tuda, who died of the plague after only a short time in his post. Eata, abbot of Melrose, became abbot of Lindisfarne during his episcopate, and probably brought Cuthbert with him to be prior; when Tuda died, Eata replaced him as bishop.

The Synod of Whitby has often been seen as a paradigm of conflict between free-spirited Celts and institutional Romans (or Anglo-Saxons), with popular sentiment on the Celtic side and Rome seen as crushing the local indigenous church and imposing its will on them. It is sometimes written about in terms that bring to mind the description in *1066 and All That* of the English Civil War as 'the utterly memorable struggle between the Cavaliers (Wrong but Wromantic) and the Roundheads (Right and Repulsive)',[6] with the Celts as the Cavaliers and the Romans as the Roundheads.

There were real differences between the churches. The most concrete were perhaps the date of Easter, the form of the tonsure for monks (the Romans shaved the crown of the head, the Irish the front), and the words used at baptism. There were also differences in church organization, in styles of religious life and in the roles and relative power of abbots and bishops. Feelings were still raw enough, when the monk of Lindisfarne wrote his Life of Cuthbert, for him to assert, against all probability, that Cuthbert received the

Petrine (that is, the Roman) tonsure when he became a monk. A saint could not be seen to have been on the side deemed wrong by the church.

The reality, however, was not black and white—a simple matter of right and wrong—and while the eventual debate was about authority, the arguments were more subtle than a question of whether one side had the authority to impose their will on the other. The division was not, at its heart, one between Celt and Roman/Anglo-Saxon, and personal factors played a large role in the timing of the eventual debate at Whitby. Aidan's personal holiness and popularity, for example, made people willing to tolerate what they saw as his misguided keeping of the Irish Easter, but he was succeeded as bishop of Lindisfarne by Finan, whom Bede describes as 'a hot-tempered man whom reproof made more obstinate'.[7] His main antagonist was not, as one might expect, a bishop imported from Rome, but an Irishman called Ronan, who had been trained in theology and law in Gaul and Italy, both of which followed Roman practices. Finan was succeeded as bishop by Colman, another Irishman, but one who held firmly to the Irish customs.

Those present at Whitby epitomized this mixture of backgrounds and beliefs. Hilda, the abbess of Whitby and therefore the host of the Synod, was an Anglo-Saxon princess, baptized in York by Paulinus in 627 and therefore brought up in the Roman tradition. When, at the age of 33, she decided to be a nun, she went first to East Anglia, still a Roman area, with the intention of going to join her sister at a convent at Chelles in Gaul; but she came under the influence of Aidan, and instead joined a new group of nuns at Hartlepool in Northumbria. She soon became abbess there. The small daughter of Oswy, Aelfflaed, was given into her charge, and Oswy then gave her land at Whitby where she founded a new monastery. She inclined towards the Irish side at the Synod, but seems to have accepted the decision made, and conformed to the Roman practice.

Oswy himself had been baptized by the Irish and spoke Irish, but also accepted the decision of the Synod. Wilfrid, leader of the Roman party, had been educated on Lindisfarne as the servant of a nobleman who had retired there to become a monk. Cedd, bishop of the East Saxons, in a Roman-influenced part of the country, had been consecrated by the Irish but served as an impartial interpreter at Whitby. Agilbert, one of Wilfrid's supporters at the Synod, a former bishop of the West Saxons and now bishop of Paris, who had ordained Wilfrid priest, had been born in Gaul but educated in Ireland.

This mixture of influences was characteristic of the church in Britain almost from the beginning. Although areas can be identified as being predominantly influenced by either Rome or Ireland, they were never watertight divisions. In the time of King Oswald (634–42), for example, East Anglia and Kent, along with Wessex, followed Rome, while the rest of the country followed Iona and therefore Ireland. Irish monks were active in both East Anglia and Wessex, however, helping with missionary work; and James the Deacon, who had come with Paulinus to Northumbria, stayed there after Edwin and his court fled south. James taught Roman practices for a further generation after the arrival of the Iona missionaries, apparently without conflict, and was present at the Synod of Whitby. Even Ireland itself was not monolithic: the southern Irish accepted the Roman Easter in 634, and most of the Irish working on the continent of Europe followed suit.

If the Easter controversy was not, at root, a conflict between two widely separated and irreconcilable traditions, what was it? Bede's account is the only one we have (and he was, of course, not present himself), but from his detailed recounting of the debate, it can be seen that the argument was much more about the unity of the church, and about how Christian practice might legitimately develop from the evidence of the scriptures and the life of the early church.

Colman, for the Irish side, claimed to follow the practice of the apostle John, handed down through Columba and the other saints of Ireland and Iona. Wilfrid took his authority from Peter and Paul, and also made great play of the fact that the church in general observed the Roman Easter: in Africa, Asia, Egypt, Greece, Italy and Gaul, this was the custom. In fact, he said, rather tactlessly (Wilfrid was not renowned for his tact), 'The only people who are stupid enough to disagree with the whole world are these Scots [i.e. the Irish] and their obstinate adherents the Picts and Britons, who inhabit only a portion of these two islands in the remote ocean.'[8] Wilfrid redeemed himself, however, by a subtle argument, accepting that John may in good faith have done as Colman claimed, but that as the faith had developed away from its Jewish roots, Christian practice had changed. As it was no longer necessary for Gentile converts to be circumcised as Timothy had been (Acts 16:3), neither need they be bound by the rules for Passover in their dating of Easter.

In the end, the king made his decision on the basis of the primacy of Peter among the saints, a primacy confirmed by the words of the Gospel: 'You are Peter, and on this rock I will build my church, and the gates of Hades will not prevail against it. I will give you the keys of the kingdom of heaven' (Matthew 16:18–19). Both Colman and Wilfrid agreed that these words were spoken by Jesus to Peter, and that no other saint, including Columba, had been given the same authority. So the king concluded that, as Peter guarded the gates of heaven, his practice should therefore be followed, in order that he might be willing to open those gates for those who died following the faith.

There was a missionary impulse behind this debate and its resolution. Easter was absolutely central to the preaching and practice of the new faith—the focal point of the whole drama of passion and resurrection, the point from which the entire calendar was calculated, and one of the few times when converts were baptized. Benedicta Ward describes it as 'the pivot of the whole of the cosmos, the central moment when reality was revealed in the face of Jesus Christ'. She continues:

Here evangelical doctrine, corporate liturgy and inner devotion were united, and in this unity [the first Anglo-Saxon Christians] discovered also their oneness with the Church in other times and places. That the missionaries who preached the Gospel to them should differ about the date on which this Paschal mystery should be celebrated was both confusing and scandalous; where external practice was not something separate from internal faith, the implications of such division were in no way trivial.[9]

This is an argument that would have appealed to Cuthbert, and perhaps it helped him to lay aside some of the practices with which he had been brought up and to accept the decision of the Synod. This didn't mean, though, that he became overnight a different person. His formation as a Christian and as a monk was firmly in the Irish tradition, and his life continued in many ways to fit this mould. Although the hagiographers try sometimes to fit him into different and, in their eyes, superior patterns, how he in fact lived continues to fit much better with the Irish pattern—a combination of genuine pastoral concern with a deep valuing of solitude, arising out of a belief in the superiority of the contemplative life.

Not everyone seems to have made the changes so graciously. Melrose, having been founded from Iona by Aidan himself, un-doubtedly followed Irish customs, as did Lindisfarne, founded from Melrose. When Bishop Colman left Lindisfarne, Bede tells us that he took with him those who shared his views, so leaving the way clear for a change. There are hints, however, that not all the monks were convinced of the necessity of following the Synod's decision. When Cuthbert came to Lindisfarne as prior, he found that 'some of the monks preferred their old way of life to the rule'.[10] While we do not know in any detail what this rule was, we do know that Cuthbert composed a rule for the house, and given that this was in the immediate aftermath of Whitby, it is likely that it included provision for the correct celebration of Easter according to Roman practice, and for the Roman form of the tonsure. Iona itself gradually came round, accepting the Roman Easter in 716 and the tonsure in 718. By the time Bede wrote his *Ecclesiastical History* in 731, only the Church in Wales still held to the old Irish customs.

The concern for the unity of the church and for the effectiveness of its missionary work, which perhaps helped Cuthbert to make this choice, is a pointer to other choices that he made throughout his life. He made them not consulting primarily his own prefer-ences, but seeking to know and follow the will of God and to serve him in and through his church. This doesn't mean that all his choices were easy to make or to carry out. We have seen how reluctant he was to be elected bishop, and it seems that even after his consecration he may have returned to his island hermitage, unable to tear himself away from his beloved island. Eata called him to Melrose, however, and this may well have been when the agreement to exchange dioceses was made. After this, it seems that Cuthbert began his active episcopal ministry, beginning immedi-ately on his journey back to Lindisfarne with healing a servant of one of the king's bodyguards.

The conflict between his deepest desires and the demands of the church and the world was something Cuthbert had already had to wrestle with as a hermit. His solitude had deepened over the years on Inner Farne. Initially the brothers came regularly to visit him, bringing him food. As time went on, however, he began to grow his own food and to talk to visitors only through the window of his hermitage. Eventually even that was blocked up, and he opened it only to give a blessing. But the world would not leave him alone. The monks were not his only visitors. Visitors, including kings and queens, came from all over Britain to ask his advice and his prayers. The church, in its admiration for hermits, wanted to use them as priests, bishops and spiritual advisers, thus risking the destruction of the life that made them admired in the first place.

Although it seems to have been awareness of his growing physical weakness and approaching death that made Cuthbert resign as bishop after only two years and return to Inner Farne, perhaps he also had a sense that he could sustain the busy, public life of a bishop for only so long. If it was his years of solitude and prayer that had made it possible to accept the task, he may have felt that his reserves were being rapidly used up, and needed to be replenished by further time in solitude. This is not an unusual pattern: Francis of Assisi, for one, alternated periods of intense and demanding activity with times of withdrawal for solitude and prayer.

Although faithfully at the service of the church, Cuthbert also held to his personal vision of calling, from his very early days as a monk in Melrose to the final decision to return to Inner Farne and solitude. He walked a fine line between the sometimes conflicting demands of the church, the religious life and his own deeper call to solitary prayer, fuelled always by a desire to live a life of 'faith working through love'.

*** *** ***

HERE AND NOW

Choice is a very strong feature of today's society and church. Having more choice is almost universally seen as a good thing, and the basis on which choices are made is often no more than 'what I want' or 'what I like'.

How do we bring God into our choices? On what basis do we believe that God makes choices within our lives? While not abdicating all responsibility by believing that our only need is to find out what God's plan for our lives is, and then follow it in every detail, how do we enter a dialogue in which God can speak to us and guide us?

What role does and could scripture play in this process?

Remembering Cuthbert and Boisil's shared reflection on John's Gospel, on 'faith working through love', we may see this as a source of nourishment for Cuthbert throughout his life. What are the formative parts of the Bible for you, the books and passages that are touchstones in times of crisis and decision?

Where there is difference in the church, how do we deal with it? Do we consciously look back to the scriptures and the traditions of the church when differences arise? Are we willing to submit our arguments to an authority and accept the outcome? Where are we willing to compromise, and where will we draw a line and not cross it?

Can we see difference as enriching and not divisive? As the Celtic and Roman/Anglo-Saxon traditions came together to create a distinctly 'English' spirituality and way of being church, can we draw on various traditions, shaping them all into a means of drawing others into the faith story by which we live?

CHAPTER 4

WHOSE FEET WILL YOU WASH?

The conflict that was a feature of the life of the church as a whole wasn't absent from the monasteries. We've already seen briefly that Cuthbert encountered problems when he moved from Melrose to be prior at Lindisfarne. Bede gives few details, but it seems that Cuthbert may have tried to tighten up on a way of life that had become slack. Not suprisingly, some of the monks resented this. We can see a glimpse of steel in Cuthbert's tactics.

Some of the monks preferred their old way of life to the rule. He overcame these by patience and forbearance, bringing them round little by little through daily example to a better frame of mind. At chapter meetings he was often worn down by bitter insults, but would put an end to the arguments simply by rising and walking out, calm and unruffled. Next day he would give the same people exactly the same admonitions, as though there had been no unpleasantness the previous day. In this way he gradually won their obedience.[1]

Cuthbert was not the only prior to suffer in this way. Ceolfrith, an almost exact contemporary of Cuthbert, was made prior of Wearmouth by its founder, Benedict Biscop. Ceolfrith's anonymous biographer tells us, 'Meanwhile Ceolfrith found his office of prior irksome… He suffered acutely from the bitter attacks of certain noblemen who could not endure regular discipline…'.[2] In fact, so difficult did he find his life there that he returned to his original monastery of Ripon, but Benedict followed him and asked him to return. Finally Ceolfrith agreed, continuing as prior and then abbot, first of Jarrow and then of the joint monastery of Wearmouth-Jarrow for many years until shortly before his death in 716.

The word 'regular' comes from the Latin *regula*, meaning 'rule'. Ceolfrith's noblemen were probably chafing under the disciplined life of a monastic rule, as did some of the Lindisfarne monks under Cuthbert's leadership. What rule would this have been? It's easy to assume that it must have been the rule of St Benedict, which, though not the first rule to be written for monks, is certainly the most enduring. Benedict lived in Italy in the sixth century, so his rule would theoretically have been available to Cuthbert and to Benedict Biscop and Ceolfrith.

In fact, the reality is far more complex. The anonymous biographer of Cuthbert says that 'he arranged our rule of life which we composed then for the first time and which we observe even to this day along with the rule of St Benedict'.[3] It isn't clear from this whether Cuthbert brought with him the rule of St Benedict, or whether it was later added to the rule that Cuthbert composed, or even whether the biographer is referring to the rule of St Benedict that we know or to the rule of Benedict Biscop at Wearmouth. The oldest surviving copy of the rule of St Benedict in Europe is in an English manuscript probably written around 700, well after Cuthbert's death; and Wilfrid, another contemporary of Cuthbert, claimed in 703 that he had himself brought monastic life into conformity with the rule of St Benedict, and that no one had previously introduced it to England. Not until the reign of Edgar in the second half of the tenth century was the rule of St Benedict imposed on all English religious houses.

We cannot, then, take Benedict's rule as the pattern for English monastic life of Cuthbert's time, so what kind of rule were they following? The answer is that each founder and subsequent leader composed a rule for their own community. We know of rules from Ireland, Spain, France and England, and the traditions of religious life in the Eastern church may also have played their part.

Archbishop Theodore of Canterbury, as a Greek monk, would have been formed in the Eastern tradition represented, for example, by the rule of St Basil. With this rich melting-pot of existing experience and influence to utilize, most founders did not start from scratch, but drew on those existing rules and on their personal experience in other religious houses. Benedict Biscop, in his last illness, told his monks: 'You must not think that the ordinances I laid down for you were the result of my own untutored invention. No, all I found best in the life of the seventeen monasteries I visited during my long and frequent pilgrimages, I stored up in my mind and have handed on to you.'[4] Sadly, no trace of this rule survives, and nor does the Lindisfarne rule of St Cuthbert, or in fact any other rule specifically composed for an English monastery. They were particular to their time and place, and when the monastery ceased to exist, the rule went with it.

Although we cannot turn to the rule followed to tell us about life in monasteries, and specifically to tell us about Cuthbert's life at Melrose and Lindisfarne, we can gain some kind of a picture from the various writings about Cuthbert and others of his century. We have little information specifically about Cuthbert— the details of daily life in the monastery were not the concern of the hagiographers—but by weaving together information from various sources, and using our imagination, we can perhaps bring into sharper focus the life that formed the context of the whole of his adult life. It is rather like trying to picture Jesus at Nazareth in the hidden years before his public ministry. As with that exercise, there is no way to be sure that the picture is accurate, but that doesn't mean it isn't worth trying.

To begin with, we must not imagine large and beautiful stone buildings such as we now see, if only in ruins, at places like Fountains or Glastonbury. The first church at Lindisfarne, built by Aidan, was wooden. It was replaced by Finan with one more suitable as the home of a bishop, but this was still wooden and, in the Irish manner, thatched with reeds. There is no evidence of a stone church at Lindisfarne before some parts of the present parish church, which may date from the ninth century. Irish monasteries usually had a number of small buildings rather than one large communal one, with separate huts providing sleeping and working space for the monks, and others as kitchen and guesthouse, all gathered around a church.

Melrose, founded from Iona by Aidan, would have been in this style, and it seems likely that, initially, Lindisfarne was too. By Cuthbert's time, however, we have a clue from Bede's writing that there was at least a common dormitory for all the monks, rather than individual cells or huts. As no one rule governed the lives of all monks, so there was no one building plan for monasteries. Excavations at Wearmouth and Jarrow, Benedict Biscop's monasteries, seem to point to a pattern of a church with public buildings arranged round a cloister, echoing the Roman secular buildings that Benedict had, no doubt, seen on his many travels. At Whitby, by contrast, archaeologists have found a number of small separate buildings.

One feature that does seem to have been common to nearly all monasteries was some kind of marker of the monastic enclosure. This may have been an earthen bank or ditch, a wall made of stone, timber, or wattle, or even a hedge of thorn bushes. Part of its function was to provide a protective barrier, but it also had a symbolic importance, marking out the monastery area as a holy place which was to be kept free from aggression. At Lindisfarne the enclosure was marked by an earthen bank, and contained not only the church and the monastic buildings, but also fields and garden.

Whatever the physical setting, certain common elements in the living of the life can be discerned. The church at the centre of the monastery was a place of corporate prayer; the cells or huts or cloister for private prayer and study; the refectory for meals in common, representative of the common life of work and recreation; and the guesthouse for hospitality.

Monks and nuns, whichever rule they followed, all came together several times a day to pray the offices—set services made up of psalms, readings (largely from the Bible, but sometimes also from the Fathers of the Church) and prayers. We know that Cuthbert was very committed to this part of the monastic life. While staying at Coldingham, despite spending all night in prayer on the beach and in the sea, he was still in the chapel at daybreak to join in the common prayer of the sisters and brothers. When he was travelling away from the monastery, he would still pray the psalms at the proper time.

There were wide variations in how the office was said and what it contained. It was still developing during this period, and there was no centralized body to lay down one authorized form. For monks and nuns, the corporate prayer of the office and their own personal prayer were closely linked. The psalms were at the heart of both and, for some, became a background prayer to everything else in life. Bede tells of Cuthbert walking around Lindisfarne, singing the psalms as he went, and talking to the monks as he met them, enquiring how they were and how their work was going.

Work was another important element in the monastic life. The larger communities would have been largely self-sufficient for all the necessities of life. They grew their own food, kept animals, baked their bread, made and mended utensils and tools, spun yarn and wove cloth. A glimpse of this aspect of the life can be seen in the story of Eosterwine, a cousin of Benedict Biscop, who was appointed abbot of Wearmouth while Benedict was on one of his journeys to Rome.

He took his share of the winnowing and threshing, the milking of the ewes and the cows; he laboured in bakehouse, garden and kitchen, taking part cheerfully and obediently in every monastery chore. He was no different when he attained to the rank and authority of abbot… Often as he went about on monastery business, he would come across the brethren at work and would quickly go and help them in whatever they were doing, putting his hand to the plough along the furrow, hammering iron into shape or wielding the winnowing-fan.[5]

Ceolfrith, too, did not exempt himself from the ordinary work of the monastery because of his rank. While training for the priesthood 'he held the office of miller-and-baker, in which he applied himself to learn and practise the priesthood's ceremonies while he ground the flour, cleaned and lit the oven and baked the loaves'.[6] This is the more striking when we realize that priests were not numerous and were therefore of high status.

Cuthbert valued manual work. When he was living on Farne as a hermit, he at first had food brought to him by the monks who visited him, but then decided that he should follow the example of the desert fathers and grow his own food. So he asked the monks to bring him, instead of food, the implements necessary to work the land, and seed so that he could grow his own wheat. The wheat failed to grow, so he tried barley instead. Although it was planted at the wrong time of year, it flourished and produced a very good crop.

In the larger monasteries, at least, along with the practical work needed to sustain daily life went more creative work, such as copying and illuminating books, decorative metalwork, study and writing. The famous *Lindisfarne Gospels* were made on the island not long after Cuthbert's death, and were probably both written and illuminated by one man—an enormous and time-consuming feat of creativity. Bede himself had as his main work in his monastery of Jarrow the writing of books; over his lifetime he wrote more than thirty. The monasteries were the main suppliers of books for the life of the church, for mission and pastoral work. They were also the most usual place for education, not just for the novice monks but also for children who did not intend to enter the monastery. Most Anglo-Saxon monasteries of any size would have had a number of children aged seven to fourteen as part of the household, there primarily to be educated but also sharing in much of the day-to-day life of the monastery.

A powerful symbol of the importance of the common life in monasteries was footwashing. It took place in church as part of the liturgy of Maundy Thursday, but also happened at other times as an expression of mutual care and service. When brothers visited Cuthbert on Farne, 'he would go out and see to their needs; he would, for instance, wash their feet in warm water'.[7] With no tap to turn on, nor boiler to produce a constant supply of warm water, this involved a considerable amount of work. The brothers would sometimes persuade Cuthbert to let them return the service. Bede tells us that he would sometimes keep his boots on for months on end without removing them, so the brothers' care must have been sorely needed.

Footwashing was also offered to guests, and was an important part of the hospitality of the monasteries. In this they followed the normal custom of the time. When Cuthbert was a bishop, he visited the house of a member of the royal bodyguard, and we are told that the first act of his host was to offer the 'formal hospitality of having his hands and feet washed'.[8]

Hospitality often took more concrete forms as well. Two stories from before Cuthbert became a monk show him both offering and receiving generous hospitality. One has him laid up with a swollen knee, when a stranger on a white horse appeared and asked if he would receive him as a guest. Cuthbert expressed his willingness, but pointed out his inability to do so because of his knee. The guest inspected his knee, gave directions for a poultice, and then rode off. Cuthbert followed the instructions and his knee was cured. He spoke of this as an encounter with an angel. In the other story, it is Cuthbert who is the traveller. He stopped at the home of a devout woman, who let him rest and pressed him to eat with her. As it was Friday and he was fasting, he refused. She tried then to persuade him to take some food with him, to eat when his fast was finished, but this too he refused.

While a monk at Ripon, Cuthbert was made guestmaster. There he encountered another angel, in the form of a guest who appeared on a snowy day. Cuthbert washed his hands and feet, and even rubbed the guest's hands with his own to warm them. He offered him food. The guest was reluctant to stay until the meal time, but Cuthbert prevailed. He fetched a table from the storehouse and went to look for bread. It was still baking, so he returned to the guest, only to find that he had disappeared, leaving not a footprint in the snow. However, three warm, freshly baked loaves now sat on the table.

This touching encounter probably took place in a separate guesthouse, either just inside or just outside the perimeter of the monastic enclosure. It seems from the literary evidence that all monasteries had some provision for guests. The one at Ripon seems to have been sparsely furnished if a table had to be fetched to enable the guest to eat, but some may have been equipped more fully. Certainly the guesthouse at Lindisfarne had beds of some sort, as one of the duties of the guestmaster there was to wash the blankets in the sea. Even Cuthbert's hermitage on Farne had a small building for guests.

The offering of hospitality had a particular religious motivation, drawn from the letter to the Hebrews: 'Do not neglect to show hospitality to strangers, for by doing that some have entertained angels without knowing it' (13:2). It was also a way in which the monasteries took part in the ordinary society of their time, offering the same hospitality to travellers as anyone would. Their enclosure was intended to protect their life, but not to cut them off from any contact with lay people. Although the sites of many monasteries may now seem remote, especially the many on coasts or islands (in about 100 miles of the coast of north-east England and south-east Scotland we know of the sites of nearly a dozen monasteries of this period), they were not necessarily so then. Much travel took place by sea, and these monasteries were often on regular sea routes. This meant that they provided convenient meeting places for nobles and church dignitaries. In fact, easy accessibility was a factor that some founders took into account when deciding on the site of their monastery. St Cronan, an Irish founder, moved his monastery after people failed to find him at the original site. 'I will not be in a desert place where guests and poor people cannot easily find me, but I will stay here in a public place,' he said.[9]

It was not only so that people could easily find them that most monks chose to live in accessible places, but so that they could go out to the people. The division now found in religious life between active, apostolic communities with a ministry outside the community, and contemplative communities whose ministry is predominantly one of prayer, is not found in early Anglo-Saxon monasticism. Most monastic houses were founded first as centres for missionary work, and these would naturally continue to offer care to those they had converted, alongside their own life of devotion.

Monasteries were the centres for pastoral care in the seventh-century church. The parish system as we now know it did not fully exist until the twelfth century, and there were relatively few churches. Those that did exist were places of private prayer, perhaps founded by a local landowner but without a priest of their own. Priests also were few and far between (in the eighth century perhaps only 20 per cent of monks were ordained), and most, if not all, lived in community of some sort—a community that served the surrounding people. This was a development from the early church pattern, which had the cathedral, with its bishop and his clergy, as the focus of prayer, pastoral service, administration, education and training of future clergy. As Christianity spread, the cathedrals could no longer serve all the Christians, and minster churches were founded on the same pattern.

'Minster' is simply the English translation of the Latin *monasterium*, 'monastery', and there is some controversy about the exact definition of a minster. Was it a small monastic community, with its members living under a monastic rule of some kind, or simply a group of secular priests living together and serving the surrounding area? The question is complicated by the fact that bishops seem to have been nervous about priests living on their own, so all were expected to gather some kind of team around them. Like monks, they prayed the office together every day, and, as in monasteries, the heads of these groups were called abbots. When monastic life was very varied, not tied to the observance of one rule or even a small number of rules, questions of definition are tricky, especially when the evidence is limited.

Another complicating factor is that we depend on Bede for much of our evidence. He had a strong belief in church unity and in uniformity of practice as evidence of that unity, so he may have deliberately emphasized similarities and ignored differences between religious houses and varying patterns of church life. Perhaps it doesn't matter much. Maybe what is more important is that the centres of worship and pastoral care were undoubtedly corporate and communal, based on a group with a common life rather than being focused on one person.

From this common life, monks and priests went out, often in twos or threes, to preach, to teach, to baptize, to visit the seriously ill and dying, and to bury the dead. Sometimes there would be a church that they could use as a base, but often they worked in the open air, perhaps gathering the people at one of the wooden or (later) stone standing crosses that characterize this period, or in private homes.

It was not only the priests who went out to do this work; although only they could administer the sacraments, celebrating the eucharist, baptizing and absolving, other monks and indeed nuns could preach and teach. We know that, from his early days in the monastery at Melrose, Cuthbert went out on preaching tours, some of which lasted several weeks, and he made a special point of going to the places that other preachers shunned 'because of their poverty and squalor'.[10]

The monastic churches were also places to which lay people came to receive the sacraments, to be taught, and sometimes also to be buried. Excavations at Wearmouth have found a large early

Christian cemetery south of the abbey church, with burials of men, women, young people and children. A study of Bede's sermons has shown that, at certain important feasts of the Christian year, he was preaching to an audience made up of more than the monks. On Holy Saturday, for example, he distinguishes between those who already receive the sacraments and those who do not yet do so—the catechumens, those under instruction before receiving baptism. These people can hardly have been monks.

Given the centrality of the monasteries in church life, it is not surprising that real authority resided in the abbot much more than in the bishop. The bishop had his liturgical role, and was necessary for the sacraments of confirmation and ordination, and to consecrate the holy oils used to anoint the sick, but most bishops were subject to the authority of the abbot, particularly when a confederation of monasteries provided a strong power base for the abbot of the leading monastery.

The double monasteries, a peculiarly English institution, provide another example of the ministry, power and influence of the leader of a monastic community. Communities made up of both men and women, they were always ruled by an abbess, drawn initially from the family of the founder and often of noble or even royal birth. The best-known of these communities was at Whitby, whose first abbess, Hilda, advised kings and princes as well as ordinary people. The choice of her monastery as the site for the Synod of 664 demonstrates her influence. Her successor, Aelfflaed, also played a decisive role in the appointment of clergy and bishops.

This Aelfflaed was a close friend of Cuthbert's. That statement would have surprised me in the early days of my coming to know Cuthbert. On the day of my encounter with Cuthbert in Durham Cathedral, I had performed a little ritual—stepping over a line of marble set in the floor near the west end of the church—almost as far as one could get from the saint's shrine near the east end. This line marked the point beyond which women were not allowed to go for several centuries. Ever since I discovered this story on my first visit to Durham as a teenager, I had taken delight in stepping over the line.

In earlier times, if some of the writings about Durham and Cuthbert's shrine are to be believed, this would have been very dangerous. They recount various stories of women who wittingly or unwittingly transgressed this rule and suffered appalling consequences. Emeloth, a small girl who lived on the opposite side of the river to the cathedral, is one of them. While playing with her friends, a ball strayed into the cathedral, and Emeloth, unaware that Cuthbert apparently forbade any female to enter his cathedral, went in to fetch it. Despite her ignorance of the rule, she went out of her mind for a while. At one time, it was not only the cathedral that was out of bounds to women but even the burial ground around it. This was the downfall of Sungeoua, who, returning from a dinner party with her husband, Gamel, took a shortcut through the burial ground because of the muddy holes in the street. Immediately she had crossed the fence on the other side of the burial ground, she collapsed and died.

These stories date from the eleventh and twelfth centuries, and are the beginning of a strange change in the saint's reputation. For over four centuries after his death there are no similar stories, and nor is there anything in his biographies to give credence to them. The opposite is true: he is shown as having good and friendly relations with various women—with Kenswith, his former nurse and foster mother; with Aebbe, abbess of Coldingham; with King Ecgfrith's queen; with Verca, abbess of Tynemouth; and, above all, with Aelfflaed, abbess of Whitby. It is noteworthy that nearly all of these women were nuns; even Ecgfrith's queen became a nun after her husband's death, with Cuthbert himself giving her the habit. Perhaps the vowed religious life offered a freedom that allowed Cuthbert to have these women as friends and confidantes.

This is an area of Cuthbert's life where it is sometimes particularly interesting and instructive to compare the same story in the anonymous Life and in Bede's Life. Bede tends to downplay the friendship with these women, about which the anonymous monk writes quite naturally. For example, the anonymous writer begins a story about how Cuthbert saved the house of his nurse and foster mother from fire, like this:

At the same time the holy man of God was invited by a certain woman called Kenswith, who is still alive, a nun and widow who had brought him up from his eighth year until manhood, when he entered the service of God. For this reason he called her mother and often visited her.[11]

Bede instead has Cuthbert happening to visit her while already on his travels, rather than responding to Kenswith's invitation.[12]

Cuthbert's visit to Aebbe and the nuns and monks at Coldingham (this was another double monastery) is also seen in a subtly different light in the two sources. In the anonymous Life, he is sent for by Aebbe and comes in response to her invitation; in Bede's Life she also invites him, but with a purpose, to 'exhort the community'.[13] Simple friendship is not enough of a reason.

The abbess Verca appears only in Bede's Life, and here he does acknowledge Cuthbert's affection for this woman. In his last illness, Cuthbert gave instructions about his burial, telling Herefrith, a Lindisfarne monk and later abbot, to bury him in a stone coffin, wrapped in a cloth about which he said: 'Abbess Verca gave it me as a present but I was loath to wear it. Out of affection for her I carefully put it aside to use as a winding-sheet.'[14]

It is Aelfflaed, however, to whom Cuthbert seems to have been closest. She was the sister of King Aldfrith of Northumbria (686–705), and in 680 succeeded Hilda as abbess of Whitby, which she ruled jointly with her mother Eanflaed until her death in 713. The story which shows her relationship with Cuthbert most clearly is found in both sources, and begins with Aelfflaed asking to meet Cuthbert. The anonymous Life adds the detail that the meeting took place on Coquet Island, a little south of

Alnmouth, a reminder that the sea was often the easiest means of travel.

Aelfflaed had various questions to ask Cuthbert, especially about her brother King Ecgfrith. She wanted to know how long he would live and who would succeed him. Cuthbert prophesied that the king would die within the next year, but that he would be succeeded by Aldfrith, the illegitimate son of Ecgfrith's father, and hence also Aelfflaed's brother. She then asked about Cuthbert himself and his future, and he revealed to her that he would be made a bishop, but only for a short time, and would then die. Then he told her to tell no one of this prophecy, and they parted. In the anonymous Life, this information is known only by one other—Hereberht, a hermit with whom Cuthbert had an especially close friendship. By showing Aelfflaed as another confidante, the author marks her out too as a particular friend. 'Saints as visionary seers, and confessors to whom all hearts are open, are privy to the hidden mysteries of the universe and the secret thoughts of many; but the saint's revelation of his own secrets marks the recipient as a particular friend.'[15] In Bede's Life, he inserts an earlier prophecy about Cuthbert's bishopric by the prior of Melrose, and Cuthbert himself occasionally hints at his future elevation to the monks at Lindisfarne; Aelfflaed loses her special position as soul friend.

Another story involving Aelfflaed finds her feasting with Cuthbert. Again Bede adds in a reason beyond simple friendship — that Cuthbert had come to consecrate a church. At the feast he had a vision of the soul of one of the monastery servants being carried to heaven. When asked the servant's name, he replied that Aelfflaed would herself name him during Mass the next day. She sent a messenger to the monastery, who initially found all safe and well, but on his return journey the messenger found that one of the brothers, Hadwald, who worked as a shepherd, had fallen from a tree and died. He returned the next day during the mass of dedication, and, as Cuthbert had foretold, Aelfflaed named Hadwald.

This part of the story again shows a difference between the attitudes of the two writers. The anonymous writer tells the story straightforwardly: Aelfflaed comes into the church with the news and names the brother, 'realizing that not only in this matter was in him a spirit of prophecy, but also perceiving in all things his apostolic foresight'.[16] Bede, on the other hand, shows the abbess in a less positive light: 'Aelfflaed hastened to the bishop, then in the middle of the dedication ceremonies, and, woman-like, acted as though stupefied, announcing, as if it were fresh news: "My lord bishop, remember at mass my servant Hadwald who died yesterday of a fall from a tree."'[17]

Given all the evidence in the biographies, and that even in Bede's interpretation of the stories Cuthbert is never less than friendly and civil to women, how did the later misogynist image arise? Rosalind Hill, in a paper given to a history conference in Oxford in 1972, puts forward a possible and, I think, convincing explanation. It rests on a change in the running of Durham Cathedral and the responsibility for the care of Cuthbert's shrine.

In 1083 a community of Benedictine monks had been established in Durham and from then on the cathedral church formed the central part of the home of a group of men committed to celibacy... Before 1083 Saint Cuthbert had been served for many years by a hereditary community of married clergy, the descendants of those who had left Lindisfarne with the saint's body in 875. Although highly respectable in a region that had felt no breath of reform in the tenth century, in the late eleventh these priests and their families appeared not merely outdated but positively scandalous by the standards of the wider church. After 1083 the monks must have been conscious of the intense resentment felt by the ousted clergy and their relatives and in their insecurity the newcomers turned to the saint himself. By publicizing a new image of Cuthbert as a misogynist and thus discrediting their married predecessors they strengthened their position in an un-welcoming environment.[18]

It is a cautionary tale. Even where there is clear evidence to the contrary, we can remake the saints in our own image and for our own ends.

* * *

HERE AND NOW

The church's ministry in Cuthbert's time was exercised far more by groups of Christians living together intentionally than by isolated individuals. How might seeing ministry as the responsibility of the entire community rather than the job of one (usually ordained) person change present patterns of ministry in the church?

How hospitable are we—as individuals, as churches, as nations? Do we see hospitality as a natural expression of our interdependence, as a way of 'entertaining angels unawares', or as a burden?

Are there parts of your own life story, of the story of your faith community, or of the Christian story, which have over the years been 'rewritten' to serve a particular purpose? How might you recover the original story, and what would be gained by doing so?

CHAPTER 5

CHRIST LIVES IN ME

It was while praying that Cuthbert saw the vision of Aidan's soul being carried up to heaven that led him to join the monastery at Melrose, and he spent the last days before his death in intense prayer in his hermitage on Farne. Prayer was the bedrock of Cuthbert's life, and we cannot understand him or learn from him without looking more closely at when and how and why he prayed.

The night-time prayer in which he saw his vision of Aidan was not a rare or special occurrence. Both of Cuthbert's biographers tell us that it was normal for him. Bede introduces the story: 'One night when his companions had gone to sleep and he was keeping watch and praying as usual …',[1] and the anonymous biographer says that 'he was spending the night in vigils according to his custom, offering abundant prayers with pure faith and with a faithful heart'.[2] It was natural for him to pray, whether as part of his normal routine or in times of need. The story of the mysterious visitor who healed the young Cuthbert's knee in the previous chapter ends with the information that 'from that time… whenever he prayed to the Lord in the times of his greatest distress, he was never denied the help of angels'.[3] His prayer was not only for his own needs. In fact, Bede makes a connection between Cuthbert's willingness to pray for others in their need and God's willingness to answer Cuthbert's prayer for his own difficulties.

One of the most striking stories about the power of Cuthbert's prayer for others is that of the monks of Tynemouth. Their monastery was built, as the name implies, at the mouth of the River Tyne, some way south of Lindisfarne, and they used to bring the timber they needed for building and repairs down the river on rafts, from some distance away. On one occasion they had just arrived opposite the monastery and were preparing to bring the rafts in to land when a westerly gale sprang up, scattering the rafts and driving them down the river towards the open sea. The monks inside the monastery tried to help, but in vain. The wind was too strong. They gathered on a rock overlooking the sea and prayed fervently for their brothers, but for a time it seemed that they would undoubtedly drown. Then Cuthbert, who was on the opposite bank of the river, joined in the prayer, and immediately the wind changed direction and blew the rafts back to the monastery, and even to a safe landing place. Bede was told this story by a monk from the monastery, who had heard it from one of the peasants who watched it all happen.

These stories come from the time before Cuthbert became a monk, but they are characteristic of his dedication to prayer throughout his life. As a monk he would have been committed to the times of corporate prayer at regular intervals throughout the day with his brothers in the monastery, but he also prayed alone. The anonymous biographer tells us that at Melrose he often prayed through the night, sometimes for several nights in a row, and Bede says that he did everything, including praying, harder than the other monks. This was not just the zeal of a young man: Bede speaks of Cuthbert praying through the night as prior of Lindisfarne, at least 15 years after he had entered the monastery at Melrose.

Cuthbert's night vigils could be very active. When staying at the monastery at Coldingham, he would, as we have seen, go down to the beach to pray at night. He would walk along the beach, singing and praying, and sometimes wading out into the sea to pray there. All of these stories of night vigils show us a man who was not content with the collective prayer of the monastery and the times of reading and study. He was hungry for God, and would use whatever free time he had in prayer and worship. Prayer became the constant thread running through his life, whether in the monastery, travelling outside, in his hermitage on Farne, or in the busyness of being a bishop.

In what is still a particular characteristic of Anglican religious life, he followed 'the contemplative amid the active life'[4] and among the many demands of life as a bishop he still put 'fastings, prayers, vigils and reading of the Scriptures'[5] in first place. The scriptures were important as motivations for prayer. They showed a God who cared for his people and would surely answer their prayers. Words from a psalm that Cuthbert would have prayed regularly are echoed in the opening of the story of the Tynemouth monks: 'This poor soul cried, and was heard by the Lord, and was saved from every trouble.'[6]

This is made explicit in another vivid story, again involving the sea. This time it is Cuthbert and two fellow monks who are in danger. They had travelled to the land of the Picts, most probably some way up the east coast of what is now Scotland, arriving after Christmas. Perhaps in over-optimism, they had not brought any supplies, relying on calm seas and favourable winds to return home soon. As soon as they had landed, however, there was a violent storm, and they were stranded, hungry and cold. Cuthbert continued to pray as the ordeal deepened. Then, as Epiphany approached, he spoke to his companions.

'Why do we remain listless and unresourceful?' he asked. 'We ought to be thinking over every possible way of saving ourselves. The land is bleak with snow, clouds lour in the sky, there is a gale raging and the sea is a fury of waves, we are dying of hunger and there is no chance of human aid. Then let us storm Heaven with prayers, asking that same Lord who parted the Red Sea and fed His people in the desert to take pity on us in our peril. I believe that, unless our faith falters, He will not let us go fasting, today of all days.'[7]

Then he took them to the bank where he usually prayed, and they found three pieces of dolphin meat, which were even ready to cook. These fed them for the next three days, after which the weather became calm and they returned home.

Cuthbert's knowledge of the Bible, of the words and stories that nourished and shaped his prayer, would have come largely through the corporate prayer of the monastery, and it is to this aspect of his prayer life that we now turn. What would the places to which he came day by day to pray with his brothers have looked like? If we could take a Tardis journey back to the seventh century and stand at the doorway of one of these small, probably wooden, churches, what would we see?

Probably what would strike us first would be what we did not see. It would take a little while for our eyes to adjust so that we could see anything much, because these churches had few, small windows and were therefore quite dark inside. Then we might be struck by the very simple shape. Few churches were of the now-traditional cross shape, with transepts forming the arms of the cross. Much more common was a simple rectangular building, tall and narrow, with a long nave and a small chancel for the altar. We would be very unlikely to see any stained glass: in fact, glass itself would be rare. Bede tells us that Benedict Biscop had to send to Gaul for glass makers when he was building the monastery at Wearmouth, around 675. There would be no rows of pews or chairs—at the most, perhaps, a few benches around the walls where the older or sick members of the community or congregation could sit. No piles of books would be stored at the back of the church, ready to be handed out for services, and there would be no organ or indeed any other musical instrument.

So what would we see? Candles certainly, perhaps placed in bronze hanging bowls suspended from the ceiling. A central lectern, where the books necessary for the services would be placed. Those who could read and sing gathered round while the others stayed at a distance around the church and joined in as they could from memory. In monasteries, the older monks had the front places nearer the lectern, with the younger ones behind them. During the long monastic services, monks would prop themselves up on something rather like crutches, while the elderly sat on simple wall-seats (hence the saying 'the weakest to the wall'). In many churches, there would be little else except the vessels needed for the eucharist, and perhaps a censer, again made from bronze, enabling incense to be burnt during services.

In more important churches and richer monasteries, there may also have been some paintings. Bede gives us a vivid picture of Benedict Biscop's frequent journeys to Rome and of the many riches that he brought back with him. He brought not just things but people—the glass makers already mentioned, stonemasons, and a singing teacher. The objects included books, relics of the saints, vestments and pictures. On his fourth trip alone, he brought back a painting of Mary, one of each of the twelve apostles, pictures of Gospel incidents, and scenes from the book of Revelation. These were all placed in the church of St Peter at Wearmouth. 'Thus all who entered the church, even those who could not read, were able, whichever way they looked, to contemplate the dear face of Christ and His saints, even if only in a picture, to put themselves more firmly in mind of the Lord's incarnation.'[8] Some of the books, those richly illustrated manuscripts of which the slightly later Lindisfarne Gospels is a particularly striking example, would also have acted as a kind of icon, with the illuminated pictures as a focus for prayer. Perhaps they would have been left open on the central lectern for just that purpose.

What kind of worship took place in these churches? As we have seen, there was no one rule that governed the lives of all monks and nuns, and neither was there one agreed pattern of common prayer. There were different patterns again for lay people, worshipping outside the monastery. The evidence for any of this is piecemeal and fragmentary. There are no complete service books until the tenth century, and the oldest surviving liturgical documents are two from around 800. Any impression must be put together from the evidence of other writings. In any case, as anyone will know who has worshipped with a church that has official written forms of corporate prayer, one book can be used in many different ways, and the style of worship can make the same content have a very different effect.

The Eucharist was common to both monks and lay people, though the style of celebration may have been rather different— more austere in the monasteries. For neither was it a daily event. Rather, it was confined to Sundays and major festivals. Various forms, from different parts of the church, were brought to this country by missionaries or collected by travelling monks. We know of at least three versions in use in the seventh century, and the oldest Anglo-Saxon books contain a mixture of Roman and Irish rites. There is little that can be identified as specifically British in liturgy, but one practice that can be so identified is that of the kindling of the new fire on Easter Eve. It was lit from a flint, not from another fire, and so was really a new fire, symbolizing the new life of the resurrection. This custom dates from the sixth century at the latest in Britain and Ireland, and was spread to the continent during the eighth century by Anglo-Saxon missionaries.

Lay people would have heard the Bible read mainly at the Eucharist. On major feasts there would also have been a homily. Bede has left us many examples, and although the earliest collection of other preachers' homilies is from the mid-tenth century, it is believed to contain much earlier material. Preachers drew heavily on the writings of the Fathers of the Church, and the most popular subject for sermons and homilies was the end of the world.

For monks there were also the offices—regular times of corporate prayer. Most often, the monks met seven times a day in fulfilment of Psalm 119:164 ('Seven times a day I praise you'): at dawn for Lauds or Mattins, followed by Prime (the first hour), then Terce (third hour), Sext (sixth hour) and None (ninth hour). These last three were short offices, taking place around 9am, midday and 3pm. Then came Vespers, traditionally at sunset, and finally Compline at the end of the day. All of these were scripture-based, with the psalms forming the major part of each office. The whole psalter would normally have been said every week. This is a link with the Egyptian roots of the monastic life: the early desert hermits sought to pray the psalter constantly, and when they came together in community their communal prayer simply continued this practice.

Other parts of the Bible did not feature much in these day-time offices, but in the night office, prayed during the night or very early in the morning, much of the Bible, especially the Old Testament, was read in sequence over the course of a year. It was not until the eighth century that a systematic means of doing this was laid down, but presumably the practice had started before then, so we can safely assume that Cuthbert heard much of the Bible read night by night in his monasteries. As prior, he would have been responsible for deciding how long the reading was; without a set lectionary the reader simply started where he had left off the night before, and went on until he was stopped. Communal meals were often accompanied by reading, usually scripturally based, and the monks also had time for their own meditative reading. The practice of *lectio divina*—holy reading—was at the heart of the monk's prayer life. All that they heard read, or read for themselves, was meant to be a spur to prayer, which should be pure (that is, without distraction), brief and frequent. Reading led into prayer, and prayer, as it waned, back into reading.

During Cuthbert's lifetime, other readings were also being added to the offices—readings from the Fathers of the Church, often commenting on the scripture, and biographies of the saints. Everything pointed in the one direction, towards God, and novelty was not seen necessarily as a virtue.

Neither was repetition seen as a problem or something to be avoided. In fact, it was a crucial element in helping the monks to commit to memory much of what they heard and prayed. Certainly after a few years in the monastery they would have known the psalms by heart, and could therefore have continued to pray them and ponder on them outside the formal times of prayer. We have Bede's picture of Cuthbert going round the monastery singing the psalms as he went, and they may also have been part of what he was praying on the beach at Coldingham. We must not imagine him in either place with a book in hand. Books being rare and expensive, memory was much more important than it is now, and the material heard day in and day out in the offices must have formed a rich treasure store of material for prayer, meditation and contemplation.

Even if they went to church other than for the Eucharist, most lay people heard much less scripture than the monks. Their offices contained less variety in general, with the same psalms repeated frequently, and these would have come to be known by heart. They would probably also have known the Creed and the Lord's Prayer. Although there were attempts during the sixth century to introduce a daily vigil service for lay people paralleling the monks' night office, at which the Bible was read, it was not popular, and only on Sundays did many people attend. Probably more people did come to the daily morning and evening prayer, made up of hymns, the regular psalms, and ending with prayers, including litanies of intercession. In the evening, incense was burned and, as the lamps were lit, a song of thanksgiving was sung, a custom that has recently been reintroduced in some Anglican prayer books. When we sing this song, the *Phos Hilaron* ('Hail gladdening light'), each Saturday evening in my own community chapel, we are part of a very ancient tradition, going back at least to the third century. While the monastic offices were generally austere and simple, those of the people had to appeal more to the senses, with hearty singing, processions and liturgical ceremonies.

The psalms and the scripture are obvious points of contact between the seventh century and our own time. Although our ways of using them may have changed, and we no longer need to commit them to memory, they are still the foundation of common prayer for many people, and a source of nourishment that can be carried over into private prayer.

Another, perhaps more surprising, point of contact is hymns. Singing in church, especially monastic churches, was only beginning to become normal during the seventh century; the early monks were very suspicious of music as part of worship. Kent and Northumbria were the first places to introduce it. There was no way of writing music down, so the only way for music to be brought from one place to another was by personal contact. One of the early teachers in Northumbria was James the Deacon, who came from Rome with Paulinus, one of the second wave of monks sent by Pope Gregory. Paulinus became bishop of York and a missionary to Northumbria. James stayed on in the north when Paulinus returned south in 633 after the death of Edwin, and was still alive in Bede's days. Wilfrid brought two singing masters from Kent to Ripon when he founded a monastery there; and rather later, in about 680, Abbot John came to Wearmouth to teach the way of singing practised at St Peter's in Rome. Monks came from other Northumbrian monasteries to learn from him, and then went back to teach in their own monastery, so Cuthbert may in his last days have heard some of Abbot John's music from Rome.

All of these teachers were passing on ways of chanting the psalms and canticles in the office, and perhaps also ways of singing in the Eucharist. Hymns were sung by monks during the office, but not at the Eucharist. There may well have been a lot of repetition, as we know of only a very small collection of hymns, 16 in all, mainly by Ambrose, and probably brought to this country by Augustine. Some of them can still be found in the English Hymnal —for example, 'Come, thou Redeemer of the Earth' (EH14) and 'O Trinity of blessed light' (EH164)—and they continue to be sung today, perhaps especially in religious communities. They are less personal and more strongly theological than many more modern hymns, with an unflinching ability to name sin and death as the enemies and God as the only creator and saviour. Constant repetition would have added them to the store of memory, where they could add another dimension to prayer, both corporate and private.

Of course, singing was not confined to official chant and hymns. Singing was part of everyday life. The story of Caedmon the illiterate cowherd at Hilda's Abbey of Whitby tells us that. He was a servant of the monastery and, unable to take his turn in singing, left the group of servants gathered one evening to entertain each other with secular songs. In a dream he was visited by a man who ordered him to sing something, and the song in praise of God the Creator that resulted from this dream is the earliest recorded in the vernacular. If it was expected that everyone could sing to entertain one another, it is likely that improvised singing was part of many people's private prayer.

I had a powerful experience of this while on retreat in 1997 on Lindisfarne. I had walked out across the island and come to a rocky part of the coastline, where I sat looking out to sea. As I sat, I began to sing, sometimes songs I already knew and sometimes a kind of mixture of plainsong and singing in tongues. I had noticed that there were a few seals bobbing up and down out to sea, but as I sang, they seemed to be coming closer and there were more of them. I'm not a very good singer, so I don't know whether they were looking to see where the terrible noise was coming from or whether they actually liked what they were hearing, but it did seem that as long as I sang, the seals were listening. I had a strong sense of continuity with the past while doing this—the sense that, strange as it seemed to me, people had done this before in this place, and seals had listened.

The very next day I was reading a book on Celtic Christianity and was amazed to discover that this improvised singing while standing on the shore was very much part of the Celtic spiritual tradition, and one that had survived for many centuries. I had a strong sense that I had been following in the footsteps of many others, perhaps even those of Cuthbert himself. It was one of those moments when time ceases to matter and centuries vanish. The common spiritual experience dissolved them and made the fellowship of the saints very real.

Perhaps Cuthbert sang to the seals from his hermitage island of Farne as well as from Lindisfarne itself. His love of prayer, evident throughout his life, eventually led him to seek greater solitude. His biographers make it clear that he did this with the permission of his community. 'After many years in the monastery he finally entered with great joy and with the goodwill of the abbot and monks into the remoter solitude he had so long sought after, thirsted after, and prayed for.'[9] It was important that he undertook this as a development of his life in community, and not to flee from it. Solitude was not to be sought as a self-willed fleeing from the wicked world or the demands of living with one another, but as a development of God's call and in the belief that, for the individual, it would be a way of drawing closer to God in order to pray more effectively for the world. Monastic life as a development of the life of the Egyptian hermits always retained a high regard for the solitary life. Benedict, in his rule, describes hermits as those who 'after long probation in a monastery, having learnt in association with many brethren how to fight against the devil, go out well-armed from the ranks of the community to the solitary combat of the desert. They are now able to live without the help of others, and by their own strength and God's assistance to fight against the temptations of mind and body.'[10]

Cuthbert's time on the isle that now bears his name was a kind of probation for this testing life. Once he had proved he was ready for it, he moved to a more remote place—Inner Farne, a true island, about seven miles by sea south-east from Lindisfarne, and one and a half miles from the nearest mainland shore.

On each island, Cuthbert built himself a simple shelter.

Nothing remains of his buildings in either place, though on St Cuthbert's Isle are the remains of three small buildings which, though medieval, may indicate the site of earlier buildings. On Farne, we have Bede's description of Cuthbert's hermitage, which consisted of two buildings—one an oratory (for prayer) and one to live in—circular in shape, built out of rough stones and peat, with roofs of timber and straw. Cuthbert seems to have been a rather slapdash builder. After his death, Aethilwald, another Lindisfarne monk, took over his hermitage but found it in very bad repair, with the walls crumbling away. He stayed there twelve years; his successor, Felgild, in his turn found that by now the hermitage was falling to pieces and had to be rebuilt from the foundations up. Bede describes Cuthbert as 'more concerned with the splendours of his heavenly than his earthly abode'.[11] He deliberately built so that he could only look out to the sky, turning his thoughts always to God. His solitude was not total; near the landing place on Farne he built a house for visiting monks to stay in. We have already seen that they visited and were treated hospitably, and that they in turn provided for some of his needs.

We have also seen that, to preserve his solitude, he chose after a time to try to grow his own food, rather than relying on the brothers to bring him bread. This becomes the setting for one of the stories that show us Cuthbert's relationship with creation, a relationship that seems to have been deepened and enriched by his solitude. When his barley ripened, birds came down and began to eat it. Cuthbert questioned them, asking why they were eating crops they had not grown. He conceded, however, that perhaps their need was greater than his, and that God had given them permission to eat the barley. If so, he would not try to stop them; but if not, then they should stop damaging other people's property. The birds flew off and did no further damage.

Another bird story is also set on Farne. This time it concerns ravens, who were found taking straw from the roof of the visitors' building to build their nests. Cuthbert rebuked them, gently at first and then, when they ignored him, more sternly. They flew off, but one returned three days later 'and finding Cuthbert digging, stood before him, with feathers outspread and head bowed low to its feet in sign of grief. Using whatever signs it could to express contrition it very humbly asked pardon.'[12] Cuthbert forgave them all, and they returned to the island with a gift for the hermit—a piece of pig's lard, which Cuthbert kept and showed to his visitors, 'inviting them to grease their shoes with it'.[13] Cuthbert seems to have had a particular love for birds of all kinds. The eider ducks that can still be seen off the Northumberland coast are known locally as 'Cuddy's ducks'—Cuthbert's ducks—and I like to think that this preserves a memory of his fondness for them.

A delight in creation was very much part of the Irish spiritual tradition. One Irish monk wrote: 'Let us adore the Lord, maker of wondrous works, great heaven bright with its angels, the white-waved sea on earth.'[14] This was not purely a love of nature for itself; Bede makes the theological point with characteristic clarity:

Not only the inhabitants of air and ocean but the sea itself... showed respect for the venerable old man. No wonder; it is hardly strange that the rest of creation should obey the wishes and commands of a man who has dedicated himself with complete sincerity to the Lord's service.[15]

The hermit's life, though, was not made up only of harmony and beauty. As we saw in the extract from Benedict's rule, the purpose of the solitary life was primarily to wrestle with evil. Farne was thought to be haunted by devils, and Cuthbert was the first person brave enough to try to live there. Bede uses the imagery of the soldier of Christ, from Ephesians 6, to describe how Cuthbert, armed only by God, routed the powers of evil and took over the island for God. But this was not the end of the battle; it continued to the end of his life. Through his perseverance he was able to stand firm and to share his experience with others who came to seek his help in their battles. In words echoing those of Christ's temptation, Bede records Cuthbert saying:

How often have the demons tried to cast me headlong from yonder rock; how often have they hurled stones as if to kill me; with one fantastic temptation after another they have sought to disillusion me into retreating from this battle-field; but they have never yet succeeded in harming either soul or body, nor do they terrify me.[16]

Despite the battles of the solitary life, Cuthbert maintained an admirable equanimity which must have been one of the most striking and helpful things experienced by those who came to him for help. The anonymous biographer says:

In all conditions he bore himself with unshaken balance, for he kept throughout the same countenance, the same spirit. At all hours he was happy and joyful, neither wearing a sad expression at the remembrance of a sin nor being elated by the loud praises of those who marvelled at his manner of life.[17]

In fact, he often used to say that the common life of the monastery was much harder, and that people should rather admire that than his life in solitude. People did feel that he had special wisdom to impart, however, and they came not only from his own monastery but from all over the country to ask for his help. They spoke to him about their sins and temptations, and 'the common troubles of humanity they were labouring under'.[18] Cuthbert was someone who could sympathize with the ordinary needs and problems of people. Bede's description of what he offered them is warm and attractive: 'No one left unconsoled, no one had to carry back the burdens he came with. Spirits that were chilled with sadness he could warm back to hope again with a pious word. Those beset with worry he brought back to thoughts of the joys of Heaven.'[19]

Once again this was within the tradition. The combination of the active and contemplative lives was highly esteemed, and the desert fathers in Egypt had always been sought out for advice even in their solitude. Cuthbert believed that the giving of advice to those in need was an activity equal in value to prayer, drawing on the two great commandments of Jesus, enjoining both love of God and love of neighbour. The solitary life was not meant to remove the hermit from fulfilling the second of these commandments.

The interior life of another is always something of a mystery, and much more so when the other lived nearly 1500 years ago and left no writings; but even then there are ways of connecting with them, of using our imagination, our empathy, our own experience, and of noticing the practices that we do have in common as well as all that is different. Our relationship with God will always be mediated and shaped by the beliefs and values of our own time and place, but at heart it is simple. It is always and everywhere the relationship of the Creator and the creature, of the teacher and the disciple, of the lover and the beloved; and the quality and reality of the relationship will be seen in its fruits—in a life lived in obedience to God, in company with and in the service of others, with the ability to both follow and to lead, sensitivity to God's promptings and constancy in prayer, whatever the circumstances.

* * *

HERE AND NOW

How do we nourish our prayer lives? Do we starve them of time and attention and the food of the scriptures, making do with scraps of time and the way of prayer we learnt years ago? Or do we gorge on endless books on prayer, on attending workshops, in the belief that somewhere is the perfect method that will make it all easy? Perhaps we can learn from Cuthbert the truth that prayer is both simple and demanding— simple because it requires only that we constantly turn to God, and demanding because in reality that constant turning is hard to do. We can also learn something about the place of the scriptures, and of memory, in prayer. Time spent in the slow reading that allows the Bible to seep into our memory, into our bones, to be drawn on at will, can never be wasted.

Solitude may also be a means of nourishing our lives of prayer. Whether it is half an hour in the early morning, the regular day away from the telephone and TV, perhaps at a local retreat house or religious community, occasional longer times of retreat or some extended periods of solitude, it brings us face to face with the reality of ourselves, of God and, often, of the evil in the world. Used rightly, it is not a soft option or an escape, and following Cuthbert's example, it should not be used as an excuse for washing our hands of the needs of others.

The help that Cuthbert offered to others is still available today, and still needed. Do you have someone who can warm your chilled spirit back to hope, who will listen to your troubles and struggles and speak God's word to you? Or perhaps you are yourself called to do this for others? From Cuthbert we can learn that this work must always be grounded in prayer, and in the humility that knows that the wisdom comes from God.

CHAPTER 6

TO GUIDE PEOPLE HEAVENWARD

There is another aspect to the story of the Tynemouth monks, which we read in the last chapter, and it shows vividly something of the background against which much of Cuthbert's work of preaching, baptizing, confirming—in other words, his work of mission—took place. It was not only Cuthbert and their fellow monks who were watching as the monks on their rafts were being swept out to sea. There were also many local peasants. Far from joining in prayer for the monks' safety, they began to jeer. When Cuthbert rebuked them and asked them to join him in prayer for the monks' safety, they refused, saying, 'Nobody is going to pray for them. Let not God raise a finger to help them! They have done away with all the old ways of worship and now nobody knows what to do.'[1]

By 'the old ways' they meant the pagan practices which had been the faith of most of the people before the coming of Christianity, and which were not rapidly replaced by the new faith. Although Bede does not give a date for this story of Cuthbert, it seems to date from before he joined the monastery at Melrose, and so is probably from around 650. More than 50 years after the arrival of Augustine and his missionaries, and much longer since the first arrival of Christianity in Britain with the Romans, paganism still had a strong hold and the conversion of the country had a long way to go.

Even in the eighth century, paganism was still identified by the church as a problem. Bede, in a commentary on the book of

Samuel, referred to those who, in his day, were still being converted from paganism, and to new churches being built where formerly idols had been worshipped. Almost at the end of that century, Alcuin rebuked the Lindisfarne monks for reading too many Nordic sagas—sagas rooted in a pagan worldview.

The process of bringing people to Christ was not a smooth or rapid one, and there were many setbacks on the way. We can see this clearly in the fact that well into the eighth century penances were being prescribed for those who clung to pagan practices, something for which there would have been no need had the practices already died out. In the later part of the seventh century, Archbishop Theodore of Canterbury laid down penances for those who sacrificed to devils or foretold the future with their aid, who ate food offered in sacrifice (a problem St Paul would have recognized: see 1 Corinthians 8), or who burned grain after a death for the well-being of the living and of the house. Archbishop Egbert, in the middle of the eighth century, prescribed five years of penance for those practising auguries and divination, and seven years for sending forth storms. He also condemned practices such as making offerings to or vows at trees, and keeping Thursdays in honour of Thor. Interestingly, Theodore was also asked for a ruling on whether altars might be hallowed or the Eucharist celebrated in churches where heathens were buried. This demonstrates very neatly the slow and ambivalent process of conversion, where known heathens might be buried in Christian churches, but where there was also a sense that this compromised the holiness of the church.

Although there are dramatic stories of mass conversions, especially through the ministry of Paulinus, there are equally stories of relapse and apostasy. Particularly in times of crisis there was a huge temptation to return to the familiar faith of previous generations. Just around the time of Cuthbert's birth, for example, after the death of Edwin, king of Northumbria, Paulinus the great missionary fled south with Edwin's widow and family. The kingdom was divided and the two kings who succeeded Edwin, Osric and Eanfrith, forsook Christianity. As the people had followed one king into the faith, so they followed his heirs out of it again. Other kings tried to hedge their bets. Redwald, king of the East Angles, who died around 624, for example, although baptized in Kent, was persuaded on his return home to maintain pagan worship as well, keeping in the same building a Christian altar and a pagan one. His son, Eorpwald, was converted by Edwin and the kingdom became Christian, but before long Eorpwald was killed by a pagan named Richbert, so the kingdom became pagan again. After three years of Richbert's rule, he was succeeded by Eorpwald's brother Sigbert, who was a Christian, so the kingdom again, and finally, became Christian. It must have been rather like the 16th century in England, during the Reformation, when the country was Catholic, Protestant, Catholic again and then Protestant under successive monarchs. Although there were always those who stood out for what they saw as the true faith, most people went with the flow of events, at least outwardly, and this is what seems to have happened in this century of conversion, as the tide of Christianity advanced unevenly and haltingly across the country.

While sometimes it was changes of ruler that affected the faith of the people, at other times it was natural calamity. Plague was a terrifying visitation, and people would revert to their former faith in the hope of averting death. Bede tells of the East Saxons in 665, for example. Under their kings Sighere and Sebbi they suffered badly from the plague. Sighere and his part of the kingdom returned to paganism. 'Hoping for protection against the plague by this means, they therefore began to rebuild the ruined temples and restore the worship of idols.'[2] Sebbi and his people, however, held to Christianity. Bishop Jaruman of Mercia was sent to Sighere and his people to recall them to the faith, and this kind of 'rescue' work was often part of the work of bishops.

Cuthbert, as a monk at Melrose, was also confronted with those who had returned to pagan practices in the face of plague, and some of his preaching tours were specifically aimed at bringing back to the faith those who had fallen away. 'Many who had the faith had profaned it by their works. Even while the plague was raging some had forgotten the mystery conferred on them in baptism and had fled to idols, as though incantations or amulets or any other diabolical rubbish could possibly avail.'[3] It was not just initial conversion that mattered, but the continuing care and nurture of those who had accepted the faith.

The Anglo-Saxon missionaries may have had a more positive attitude than the Celtic to the existing beliefs and culture of the people to whom they preached. The Celts tended to see a more radical separation of sacred and secular, pagan and Christian, and for them conversion entailed a dramatic turning away from previous beliefs. The Anglo-Saxon mind was perhaps more pragmatic, seeing the good already present in the society that they sought to convert. 'Already among the pagan Anglo-Saxons there were ideas and ideals that would be absorbed into the new Christian teaching,' writes Benedicta Ward: 'a longing for hope, love of journeys, a sense of community, of life in the kin-group, a fundamental love of one's lord as one's greatest friend, an instinct for splendour, and a feeling for the precariousness of life.'[4]

These different approaches were reflected in different missionary methods. The stories of the Irish saints are full of dramatic confrontation—the destruction of pagan temples and idols, and challenges to pagan priests to contests of power. They would sometimes deliberately put themselves into danger so that their deliverance by God might astound and convert their pagan onlookers. They looked for a total rejection of their converts' past.

The Anglo-Saxons, drawing more on the Roman model, and especially on Pope Gregory, who sent Augustine to these islands, leaned more to a step-by-step approach, taking what was good in the culture of their listeners, converting the old temples for Christian worship, and so organizing the calendar that Christian feasts took the place of pagan festivals. According to Bede,

Christmas was now celebrated on what had been Modranect, the night of the mothers, and Easter was linked to Eostre, an Anglo-Saxon spring goddess. Gregory put great store by bringing people into the faith. He wrote:

Certain it is that it is a greater miracle, by preaching of the word and virtue of prayer, to convert a sinner than to raise up a dead man: for in the one, that flesh is raised up which again shall die; but in the other, he is brought from death which shall live for ever.[5]

In this process, the Anglo-Saxons were happy to draw on reason. One of the most famous stories in Bede's *Ecclesiastical History* is of the final conversion of Edwin. The king summoned a council of his advisers and friends, in order to discuss the new faith and to decide whether they should embrace it. One of these friends used the vivid image of a banqueting hall in the winter. Inside, all was warmth and comfort; outside, winter storms raged. He compared what their existing faith could tell them about human life, and of what happened after death, to a sparrow who flew into the hall through one door and out through another. For a few brief moments the bird was safe from the winter storms, but then returned into the darkness from which it had come. This was like human life on earth: what came before and what came after were unknown. If the new faith could reveal more certain knowledge of these great questions, it seemed to him only right that they should follow it.

Another more cynical argument came from Coifi, the pagan high priest. He argued that if the gods he had served really had power, they should have ensured that he, Coifi, would be more successful and more favoured by the king than in reality he had been. He had devoted himself to the service of these gods, yet many had been more highly honoured. He concluded that 'the religion that we have hitherto professed seems valueless and powerless'.[6] He too was in favour of the new religion. Edwin, together with all the nobility of his kingdom and many of the people, was baptized in York on Easter Day 627.

Although looking at just this one story makes the conversion seem dramatic, in fact the process had been a longer one, and is perhaps a good model of what must often have been the case in the early days of the missionaries. They were not coming to a people who had no religion already, but to those who had a faith and who had to be persuaded to abandon it and take on instead what may have seemed strange and foreign.

Edwin's conversion began with his marriage, which was, as was usual for royalty, a means of cementing an alliance, in this case between Northumbria and Kent. As Kent was where Augustine and his monks had landed and set up their first church, it was Christian before most of the rest of the country. Edwin was to marry Ethelberga, the king's daughter, but was told that a Christian princess could not marry a heathen. Edwin promised that he would not prevent Ethelberga from practising her Christian faith, and that he would himself investigate the claims of this faith. Paulinus was consecrated bishop and sent with Ethelberga to act as chaplain to the queen and her household, and to work for the conversion of the king and of Northumbria.

The next development was the king's safe escape from an assassin sent by a rival king and, on the same day, which was Easter Day, the queen's safe delivery of a daughter, Eanfled. Edwin promised that if God would give him victory over Cuichelm, who had sent the assassin, he would become a Christian, and as a pledge he gave his daughter to be baptized. On return from his successful campaign against Cuichelm, Edwin asked to be instructed by Paulinus and to have time to discuss with his counsellors and friends the way forward. During this time of reflection, he also received a letter from Pope Boniface, who wrote also to Ethelberga, urging her to use her influence to aid her husband's conversion. It is at this point that the story of the sparrow comes. Edwin took very seriously such a life-changing decision. Bede tells us that he 'was by nature a wise and prudent man, and often sat alone in silence for long periods, turning over in his mind what he should do, and which religion he should follow'.[7]

Although the stories we have tend to be of important people such as kings, and it was traditional that the people followed the king into (and, as we have seen, sometimes out of) faith, this was in reality only one of the missionary strategies followed by the Christians of seventh-century England. Aidan, for example, was well known for travelling around on foot whenever possible and stopping to talk to everyone he met, whether rich or poor, nobility or peasant. If they were not already Christian, he urged them to be baptized; if they were, he would speak to them of the Christian life, strengthening their faith and building it up. As bishop in Northumbria, Aidan was often accompanied by Oswald, the king, who acted as interpreter—a striking example of how closely kings and bishops could work together for the conversion of their people. This was obviously a slower method of conversion than that of mass baptisms following the conversion of the king; perhaps it led to less chance of falling away in times of difficulty, though the lack of priests, especially in remote areas, made continuing nurture difficult, and the temptation to return to pagan ways was always there.

Cuthbert, whose entry into religious life had been inspired by a vision of Aidan, seems to have followed his missionary methods, making many journeys on which he preached the word to individuals and to small groups. Like Aidan, he rarely went alone, but with one or more companions: evangelism was not a solitary activity, but a communal one. The fact that most of the missionaries were monks, living in community, must have made it quite natural to band together for this work, and perhaps such groups formed something like a travelling monastery. As a bishop, for example, one of his journeys took Cuthbert to the village of a man named Sibba, near the River Tweed. He came 'with a company of people piously singing psalms and hymns'.[8]

Earlier, as an ordinary monk, Cuthbert's groups were smaller. We saw how he went to the Picts with two other monks; another story shows him going along the River Teviot with only one boy as companion. Although most of Cuthbert's journeys were fairly local, as a bishop he went further afield, to places so remote that there were no church buildings, and Cuthbert and his company had to sleep in tents. In such places it would have been necessary to take everything needed for ministry, hence the provision of small travelling altars such as the one that is still kept in Durham among the relics of Cuthbert. Small gospel books and pocket versions of the liturgy, containing the prayers of the mass, a selection of readings, and the order of baptism, of which we have later examples, must also have been available to these travelling missionaries of earlier days.

Although he was based in Lindisfarne, there are a number of stories from a journey Cuthbert made which took him to Hexham, in the heart of Northumbria, and then across to Carlisle, near the west coast. He kept his concern for each individual even on these long and demanding journeys. Once, when the plague was ravaging the country, he set out to comfort the people of his diocese. 'In one village he exhorted everyone he found and said to the priest, "Do you suppose there is anyone else left in the place who needs visiting and speaking to, or can I now move on to the next?"'[9] The priest looked around and noticed a woman at a distance. One of her sons had already died of the plague and the other was dying in her arms. Cuthbert immediately went to her, blessed the boy, kissed him, and promised the grieving mother that he would live, and that no more of her family would die. The boy was healed, and Cuthbert's prophecy proved true.

Cuthbert combined this concern for the needs of the ordinary people with a ministry to the powerful, to the rulers. He travelled to Carlisle on one occasion in order to be with the queen of King Ecgfrith, who had gone to fight against the Picts. Ecgfrith, as we have seen, was the brother of Aelfflaed, abbess of Whitby and

Cuthbert's close friend, to whom Cuthbert had prophesied her brother's death. The queen was staying in her sister's convent. While being shown the city walls and a Roman fountain built into them, Cuthbert had a vision by which he suspected that the king had been killed. The next day was a Sunday and, as bishop, he had been asked to dedicate the chapel of a neighbouring monastery. A small detail gives us a clue to the power of his preaching: Bede tells us that after the sermon 'as the congregation were expressing their approval',[10] Cuthbert began to warn them of calamity to come. The next day, news came from the battlefield that the king and his bodyguard had indeed been killed at the very time that Cuthbert had seen the vision.

Whether king or commoner, baptism was the universal means of entry into the church, and a very important part of the work of priests. In the early church it was normal for adults asking for baptism to undergo a lengthy period of instruction, and we see something of this in the story of Edwin's conversion. Infants and children would normally be baptized as part of a family group, though again Edwin's story shows us that this wasn't always the case. Our period is one when the practice of baptism was changing, and we cannot paint a uniform picture of how it happened. Probably only a minority of baptisms took place in church. Church buildings were few and far between, and many people, especially in largely pagan areas, would have been a long way from one. Priests would baptize in private houses, and, where many people were baptized at once, rivers were sometimes used.

After Edwin's conversion, Paulinus was free to preach throughout Northumbria, and many responded to his message. Bede tells how Paulinus spent 36 days at the royal palace at Yeavering, on the northern edge of the Cheviots, instructing those who wanted to be baptized, and baptizing them in the River Glen. People came from all the surrounding countryside, and Paulinus spent each day, from dawn to dusk, at this task. He frequently did the same at another royal residence near Catterick, baptizing in the River

Swale. Bede specifically says that he did this because 'it had not been possible to build any churches or chapels for Baptism in those parts'.[11]

When someone important was to be baptized, a church might be built specially for the ceremony. Edwin, with his nobles, was baptized in a timber church, dedicated to St Peter the Apostle, which he had had built at York during the time he was receiving instruction. He later arranged for a larger stone basilica to be built on the same site, thought to be near the present Minster. The majority of baptisms, however, happened where people were. As the monks and missionaries went out to the countryside and villages to find people to whom to preach, so, when their word bore fruit, they baptized them there. Some of these travelling priests may have taken some kind of font with them, as Cuthbert took a travelling altar, but many must have borrowed something suitable from the household in which they were staying. This kind of missionary work also made necessary a much shorter period of instruction than had been normal. When a priest or bishop might not come that way again for a year or more, it was more important to bring people into the kingdom when they desired it than to keep the customs that had grown up in churches in more urban settings.

Those baptized in rivers were probably totally immersed; others might have stood in a large container and had water poured over their head so that it streamed down their body. In either case it was a dramatic ceremony that marked a real change in the life of the convert. Confirmation, then as now, was conferred by a bishop laying on hands, and usually took place separately unless a bishop was present at the baptism.

The continuing care of the converts was also largely in the hands of monks, as we have seen, and those running the minster churches. Where there was no church building, standing crosses in the open air became meeting places, perhaps for baptism and certainly for instruction and worship. The first cross to be raised in Bernicia, one of the two kingdoms of Northumbria, was the wooden cross raised by Oswald before the battle of Heavenfield, at which he defeated a pagan army, in 633 or 634. Stone crosses became normal quite rapidly. Cuthbert, before his death on Farne, asked to be buried near to the stone cross to the south of his oratory. This may well have been very simple—perhaps just a slab in the shape of a cross, rather than the elaborately carved crosses that have survived from around that period. In the intricacy of their carving, they echo the manuscripts that were also being produced at the time. Geometric interlacing patterns and figures of the saints make them both beautiful and instructive, and they could well have been used for teaching purposes by travelling preachers.

Perhaps the best-known and most magnificent of crosses to have survived is the one at Ruthwell in Dumfriesshire. It is from a little after Cuthbert's time, probably the second quarter of the eighth century. It is decorated with vine leaves, inhabited by figures, a type of ornament that comes from the Mediterranean rather than from local manuscripts. Biblical scenes include John the Baptist, Christ in Judgment, the Flight into Egypt, the Visitation, the Annunciation, the Crucifixion and Mary Magdalene washing Christ's feet. It would be possible to base many sermons and much teaching around one or more of these images. In addition, there was a scene from monastic history, showing Saints Paul and Anthony, two of the early desert fathers from Egypt, breaking bread together. It is a good summary of the spirituality of the church of Northumbria—based firmly on the Bible, with strong monastic roots, and drawing when needed on the civilization of the Mediterranean.

The crosses were not only places to meet when a priest or bishop came on a tour of the area, but also a focus for the daily prayer of the people. Well after Cuthbert's time, in the eighth century, an English nun in Germany wrote, 'On the estates of nobles and good men of the Saxon race, it is the custom to have a cross, which is dedicated to our Lord and held in great reverence, erected on some prominent spot for the convenience of those who wish to pray daily before it.'[12] The prominent spots included, in Northumbria, places near harbours, on Roman roads and at natural meeting places for sheep-farmers. Place names including 'cross' may well indicate such places, even today.

The cross was important to the Christians of Cuthbert's day, not just for its obvious role in redemption but for a more practical reason linked to their recent past as pagans. The cross was seen as a very important weapon in the fight against demons. No one doubted the reality of these manifestations of evil, and it was important that the new faith could offer the same or better protection than the old—hence the centrality of miracles for Christian writers, even in such works as Bede's *Ecclesiastical History*. A writer says of Bede:

He is still a product of his age, an age steeped in paganism, superstition and belief in the efficacy of magic, charms and incantations... Indeed there are pagan overtones in some of the miracles Bede himself records and a touch of magic in the wonder-working cures of the saint's relics. Perhaps this is intentional, Bede wishing to wean his hearers from a belief in cures effected by pagan magic to cures effected by the Christian God.[13]

There are several stories of Cuthbert fighting both real and illusory fires that broke out in villages where he was preaching. It has been suggested that the recording of these stories is connected to the pagan god Thor, god of thunder and lightning and hence of fires. If a pagan god was seeking to hinder the work of the saint, the hagiographer had to be able to show that his power was greater, and that the Christian God, through Cuthbert's prayer, could overcome pagan powers.

We need to know the background of the readers to understand why writers wrote what they wrote, just as a knowledge of the churches to which Paul wrote his letters helps us to understand his arguments. The pagan background of many Christians of

Cuthbert's time, either personally or in the previous generation, makes understandable the emphasis given to miracles of all kinds in the Lives of the saints. The world was a dangerous place, with little protection against illness of body and mind, against the effects of poor weather on harvests, against natural disaster and human violence. Any faith that hoped to capture the hearts and minds of people living in this context had to offer a better and more lasting hope than their existing faith.

The image of the sparrow that Bede records does just this, offering knowledge of what had previously been unknown and shining light into dark places. Did it really happen like this? After all, the story was not written down until more than 100 years after it was supposed to have happened. Perhaps it doesn't matter particularly. It spoke to the people of its day, and it still speaks to us, of something that is true—that the Christian faith does offer an assurance of what happens outside the brief period of our life in the warmth of the banqueting hall. Peter Hunter Blair reflects:

Bede, like all great historians, was an artist… the kind of truth which his account of the conversion brings to us is the kind of truth which we learn from Renoir or Mozart, rather than from computerized statistics… The flight of the sparrow expressed in vivid, simple terms a whole philosophy of life to be overthrown, like the images of the heathen temple, by those who accepted Christianity, and this for Bede was the truth that mattered most.[14]

* * *

HERE AND NOW

In the work of mission, Cuthbert, like many of his contemporaries, was tireless in going to where the people were in order to bring them the good news. It would have been much more comfortable for him to stay in his monastery and wait for people to come to him, but his zeal for the gospel drove him out, especially to those who were not visited by anyone else. How might this example inspire us in our work of mission today? Who are the people in 'remote places'—not necessarily geographically remote—to whom we should be going?

Cuthbert converted people from paganism to Christianity. What do the people we meet at work, at leisure, as neighbours, believe in today? Often people who say, 'I'm not religious' mean that they don't go to church, but they do reflect on ultimate questions, on values, on what comes before and after the sparrow's flight through the banqueting hall. How can we respect their honest questioning, while boldly offering something better?

We rightly see conversion today as an individual decision, and would not expect whole countries or people groups to be converted because their ruler is, but who are the 'kings' whose conversion will influence others to take seriously the claims of Christianity? Who are the missionaries to people of power and influence, and how do they work in contexts of great wealth, enormous power and many possibilities of corruption, without compromising their own faith?

CHAPTER 7

'A GREAT, BROAD HAND'

Miracles were important during a saint's life as a guarantee that he or she was favoured by God. Gregory the Great, the Pope who sent Augustine, is recorded as teaching that miracles were above all granted 'to those who instruct the pagans, and so, the more gloriously and frequently they are manifested in these lands, the more convincing they become as teachers'.[1] Cuthbert's life was marked by miracles, some done for him, many others done through him. As we have seen in Chapter 4, before entering the monastery, his knee was healed by a stranger whom his biographers identify as an angel.[2] On various occasions he was provided with food, whether by another angel,[3] by an eagle,[4] or by his horse, which found 'a warm loaf and meat carefully wrapped up in a linen cloth' while itself eating part of the thatch of a shelter.[5]

The context of miracles is always prayer, whether it is directly connected with the miraculous event, as when Cuthbert was healed of the plague by the prayers of his fellow monks at Melrose,[6] or when the prayers of Cuthbert and the monks of Lindisfarne enabled him to find water on the solid rock of Farne. 'Without a doubt,' writes Bede, 'it was the prayers of the saint that had brought forth water from ground of the driest, hardest kind.'[7]

There are several accounts of Cuthbert turning away fires, and there is also a story of him being enabled to lift, with the help of angels, stones that four men together could hardly lift, when he was building his hermitage.[8] The anonymous biographer doesn't mention angels, but does include the vivid touch that the four monks who had been asked to bring the largest stone to Cuthbert 'left it behind half-way so as not to destroy his cart nor injure themselves'.[9]

Most of Cuthbert's recorded miracles, however, are of healing. His biographers are careful to stress the role of faith in these miracles; they are set firmly in the context of Christianity and are not magical. It was important to distinguish healing by the Christian God from that which the pagan gods could offer. When the anonymous biographer tells the story of the healing of Cuthbert's knee by the angel, he says, 'After a few days he was healed according to his faith...'[10] Bede has two stories with a sophisticated understanding of the relationship of faith to healing. One concerns Aelfflaed, who, during a long illness, thought of Cuthbert and wished that she had something of his, believing that she would surely be cured by it. Shortly afterwards a linen cincture, or sash, arrived from the saint; she wrapped it around herself and within two days was completely cured. Shortly afterwards one of her nuns had excruciating pains in her head, and the cincture cured her too—but then it disappeared. Bede says that this was God's doing:

By those two miracles of healing he manifested Cuthbert's holiness to the faithful, and then removed the cincture lest it should lead the faithless to doubt such sanctity. Had it been allowed to remain, the sick would have flocked to it and if anyone through lack of merit were left uncured, the fact would be taken not as a proof of that person's unworthiness, but as a reason for disparaging the relic.[11]

This story is a good example of Bede's care to give the sources of many of his stories. He tells his readers that Aelfflaed had told this story to Herefrith, a priest of Lindisfarne, who in turn had told it to Bede. His inclusion of names of people and places, when he knew them, adds a vivid and personal touch, reminiscent of some of the Gospel stories where those who appear briefly are made more memorable by the use of their name or place—Zacchaeus, Bartimaeus, the Samaritan woman, Salome. Hence we have stories of Cuthbert healing the wife of Hemma, a gesith (a high-ranking companion of the king) of Kintis; a Lindisfarne monk, Walhstod; and a servant of the gesith Sibba, who lived near the River Tweed.

The second story about the role of faith in healing shows that nuns did not have a monopoly on the necessary faith. It tells of the sheriff (local official) Hildmer, who was dangerously ill. His friends all came to visit him, and one of them remembered that he had a piece of bread, blessed by Cuthbert, in his pocket. '"I am sure this will restore him to health," he said, "unless our slowness to believe prevents it."'[12] After an earnest discussion, the friends concluded that they all believed that Hildmer could be healed by the bread, so they filled a cup with water, dropped into it a small piece of the bread, and gave it to him to drink. Immediately the pain left him, and soon he was entirely healed. Bede concludes that this moved 'all who saw or heard of the unexpected recovery to praise Cuthbert's holiness and marvel at the strength and sincerity of Hildmer's faith'.[13]

Both of these stories show Cuthbert healing from a distance, through items that he had touched or blessed, but he also healed directly, through prayer, laying on of hands, anointing with chrism or oil, or the use of blessed water. This healing could be of the mind as well as the body. An earlier story tells of the healing of Hildmer's wife, who was thought to be possessed by a devil. Hildmer came to Cuthbert to ask his help, but was too ashamed of his wife's condition to specify what was troubling her. He said only that she was likely to die. But on the way to Hildmer's home Cuthbert perceived what her illness was, and reassured Hildmer that his wife would have been healed before they reached his home. As they approached the house, she did indeed come rushing out to meet them, restored to health. Bede puts into Cuthbert's mouth reassuring words for those who would, like Hildmer, believe that this illness afflicted only those who had displeased God: 'It is not only the wicked who are stricken down in this way. God, in his inscrutable designs, sometimes lets the innocent in this world be blighted by the devil, in mind as well as in body.'[14]

Here we see a prophetic gift linked to that of healing: Cuthbert was able to see what was about to happen. This was not the only example of this gift in Cuthbert's life. When he was a young monk at Melrose, the abbot Boisil prophesied his own death, and during his last week of life unfolded to Cuthbert much of his future life. As we saw in the last chapter, Cuthbert saw in a vision the disaster that was about to befall King Ecgfrith. Bede gives a dramatic description of this event. Cuthbert, he says, 'was suddenly disturbed in spirit. He leaned heavily on his staff, turned his face dolefully to the wall, then straightening himself and looking up to the sky he sighed deeply and said almost in a whisper: "Perhaps at this moment the battle is being decided."'[15]

The next day, in warning the people to whom he preached to be prepared for disaster, he told a story about another example of his prophetic awareness of approaching danger. One Christmas when he was living on Farne, some of the monks came over to persuade him to join them in celebrating the feast. During the meal he several times warned them of some impending danger. The brothers were initially impatient and urged him to enjoy himself on this great feast day, but eventually they were convinced by his repeated warnings, although he himself was not clear what the danger consisted of. He said to the congregation, 'I must confess I knew as little as they did whether some new temptation would attack us or not, but I felt an instinctive warning that one should be on constant guard against sudden storms of temptation.'[16] In this case the disaster was the plague, which broke out in the Lindisfarne monastery, and which lasted for a whole year, wiping out almost the entire community.

Prophecy is here presented more as an intuitive awareness of what is happening or about to happen than a chapter-and-verse prediction of some future event, but there are examples of this more precise kind of prophecy too. Perhaps the most touching happened in Carlisle, on another visit made by Cuthbert as bishop. While there, he met a hermit called Hereberht, who lived on an island in a lake. They had long been friends, and Hereberht had visited Cuthbert regularly to seek his advice on the spiritual life. While they were speaking, Cuthbert advised Hereberht to ask now anything he needed to ask. This would be their last meeting, because Cuthbert knew that he would soon die. Hereberht was naturally very upset, and begged Cuthbert to ask God that they might die at the same time, united in death as they had been in life. Cuthbert prayed fervently, and was assured that his prayer would be answered. So he left Hereberht reassured, and Bede records that they did indeed die at the same time, 'and were soon carried to the celestial kingdom by an angel host, to be united with each other in the beatific vision'.[17]

It must have been shortly after this that Cuthbert resigned as bishop and returned to his hermitage on Farne, to what Bede describes as 'his beloved life of solitary conflict'.[18] The anonymous monk gives a very brief account of Cuthbert's death, but Bede quotes at length from an account by Herefrith, the same priest who had told him of the healing of Aelfflaed and one of her nuns. It is a very moving account, which shows clearly Cuthbert's deep love of solitude, and the spiritual conflict which was at the heart of that solitude.

After two months on Farne, he fell ill. This illness lasted for three weeks (in another of Bede's touches of detail, we know that this was from a Wednesday to a Wednesday). Herefrith begged Cuthbert to allow some brothers to stay with him, to care for him in his dying days, but he refused, saying that God would show them when to return. A storm prevented their reaching the island again for five days, during which they kept a constant prayer vigil. When they returned, they found Cuthbert in the simple guest house, near the landing place. He was drained and had obviously suffered much. Herefrith heated some water and washed one of his feet which needed attention, and tried to make him take some warm wine. Then Cuthbert revealed to him that he had suffered both physically and through temptation. He had remained in the same place and position for the whole five days, eating only half of an onion. Herefrith describes this ordeal as Cuthbert's final purification and testing.

Now Cuthbert allowed himself to be cared for, and several brothers stayed on Farne with him, while others, including Herefrith, visited regularly. When he knew he was about to die, Cuthbert asked to be taken back to his hermitage. He was too weak to walk, so they carried him back. It was at this time that Wahlstod was healed. Herefrith now stayed with Cuthbert until he died. Cuthbert continued to pray, and at the time of night prayer he received communion. Then 'he raised his eyes heavenwards, stretched out his arms aloft, and with his mind rapt in the praise of the Lord sent forth his spirit to the bliss of Paradise'.[19] One of the monks on Farne immediately lit two candles and went up to a piece of high ground with them, so that the brothers on Lindisfarne would know that Cuthbert had died. It was 20 March 687. The brother in the monastery watch-tower immediately went to the church where the monks were saying the night office and told them the sad news.

Although Cuthbert had asked to be buried on Farne, predicting that many would flock to his tomb, and that it would be much less trouble to the monks to have his burial place away from the monastery, they had prevailed on him to agree to be taken back to Lindisfarne and be buried there. So, says Herefrith:

We placed the body of our venerable father in the boat and bore it across to Lindisfarne, where it was received by choirs of singers and a great crowd that had turned out to meet it. It was buried in a stone coffin on the right-hand side of the altar in the church of the Blessed Apostle Peter.[20]

Cuthbert's burial was opulent, and we may wonder what he made of such extravagance. Although he had, before his death, asked to be buried wrapped in a cloth given him by Abbess Verca, and in a stone coffin given by Abbot Cudda, that was the extent of his care for his body after death. In fact, the monks clothed him in magnificent vestments, including a white dalmatic, a chasuble made of silk, and an alb embroidered with gold thread. The gold and garnet cross that still survives was hung around his neck. A consecrated communion wafer was placed on his chest, and shoes on his feet; then he was wrapped in a waxed cloth, probably the one given him by Abbess Verca, and placed in the stone coffin. In the wooden church of St Peter he was buried near Aidan, whose death had sparked off his vocation. Neither this church nor the stone one that succeeded it survives, but it seems probable that the twelfth-century priory church whose remains still stand was built on the same site, so we can imagine there the crowds of pilgrims who came to pray at the saint's shrine.

As the saint had predicted, both pilgrims and others flocked to the island. He had worried that fugitives would 'flee for refuge to my body' and that 'you will be constrained to intercede very often with the powers of this world on behalf of such men'.[21] Certainly by the middle of the next century, we have evidence that the church had become a place of religious sanctuary, but most of the people who crossed over to Lindisfarne and came to the church of St Peter sought healing rather than sanctuary. Cuthbert's prayers were as effective in death as they had been in life, and his hands were still powerful to heal.

Bede, in the *Ecclesiastical History*, tells the story of Badudegn, the guest brother of the monastery, who suffered what sounds like a stroke. He went to Cuthbert's tomb and prostrated himself before it, praying that God would, at Cuthbert's intercession, either heal him or give him grace to bear his illness with patience.

As he prayed he fell into a deep sleep, and... seemed to feel a great, broad hand rest on the seat of the pain in his head. At this touch, the entire area

*of his body affected by the disease was gradually eased of its pain, and
health was restored right down to the feet.*[22]

Sometimes there was a pleasing symmetry in the means used to
heal a particular disease. A young monk suffering from paralysis
had been sent by his abbot to Lindisfarne because the monastery
had some skilled doctors among its monks, but their skills could
not halt the progress of the disease, and in the end the young
monk was totally paralysed. Then he turned to Cuthbert, and
asked that one of Cuthbert's garments be brought to him. His
servant brought the shoes in which Cuthbert had been buried
(later removed from his coffin), and put them on the young man's
feet at sunset. He fell asleep, but those who watched over him saw
life gradually returning to his body, beginning at the feet. When
the bell for the night office rang, he woke and sat up, completely
cured. In the morning he 'went round the holy places, praying and
offering the sacrifice of praise to his Saviour'.[23]

Items associated with Cuthbert—clothing, earth from the pit in
which the water used to wash his body had been poured, hair, or
leather that had covered gaps in his cell walls on Farne—were also
used in healing, both on Lindisfarne itself and elsewhere.

Some of these items had become available as relics some time
after Cuthbert's death. It was eleven years after his death and
burial, and the monks, expecting that by now his body would
have entirely decayed, wished to place his bones in a light coffin
above ground so that they could be better venerated. The bishop,
Eadberht, gave his consent, and so, on 20 March 698, they dug
up and opened the stone coffin. To their amazement they found
Cuthbert's body 'completely intact, looking as though still alive,
and the joints of the limbs still flexible. It seemed not dead but
sleeping'.[24] The vestments likewise had not decayed but were still
unfaded and crisp. The monks took some of the vestments to
show the bishop, who was spending Lent in retreat on St
Cuthbert's Isle. He kissed them with great devotion, and told the

monks to put new vestments on the body and to replace it in the new wooden coffin that they had prepared for it. Parts of this coffin, carved with figures of saints, can be seen in the Treasury of Durham Cathedral. The chasuble that had been removed by the monks, and the shoes, were displayed beside the shrine. The great miracle of the incorrupt body was the final proof of Cuthbert's sanctity, and established him as the greatest of the northern saints.

In the world of the seventh-century Christian, the physical was very important, so it was the saint's body, or items that had been in close physical contact with it, which were responsible for most of the miracles recorded. Something tangible was needed to convey the saint's power and God's favour. The preservation of Cuthbert's body from decay was thus a clear sign of God's favour to him, and played a very important part in his cult. There was no central church process for declaring people to be saints: cults grew up locally and were nourished and authenticated by miracles.

The miracles themselves, however, pose some problems for today's reader. Some seem to be explicable by non-supernatural means—for example, the cure of Cuthbert's knee by what seems the very sensible means of a poultice, or his ability to predict the end of a storm, which could be ascribed to his many years' experience of the Northumbrian coast. Others are recorded with the clear purpose of teaching a lesson, such as the occasion when the devil raised up a phantom fire while Cuthbert was preaching, distracting the listeners from his sermon as they tried in vain to extinguish it. The lesson was clear: do not be distracted from the word of God by the stratagems of the devil. Still other miracles are very clearly based on biblical incidents or the lives of earlier saints: the power of his clothing recalls that of St Paul (Acts 19:11–12), the exorcisms echo those of Jesus, and one miracle in which an eagle brought fish to Cuthbert and his companion is like an incident in the life of St Paul of Egypt, an early hermit, when a raven brought food to him and his companion Antony.[25]

For the writers of the time, however, this apparent lack of

originality was not a problem but a strength. In their writing they deliberately make parallels and evoke resonances with scripture and earlier saints' Lives, so we must not think that we have caught them out in something that detracts from the power of the stories. Indeed, the stories gain much of their strength from their connection to the tradition. Rollason writes, 'The point being made here by the writers is that Cuthbert's miracles revealed the working of the Holy Spirit in all the saints and in biblical incidents also, and thus what counted was their similarity to the miracles of earlier saints and biblical personages.'[26] The writers are not primarily concerned with the factual reality of every miracle recorded, but rather with showing what kind of person the saint was, and how he was part of a long tradition of servants of God.

The miracles of the saints were not always solely concerned with the healing of individuals. Sometimes there was also a political dimension. Bede records three miracles of Aidan. In one he gives a phial of oil to those sent to Kent to collect Eanflaed, Edwin's daughter, for her marriage to King Oswy. They were to pour it on to the sea if a storm arose, and the sea would be calmed. So God's power smooths the way to this political alliance. In the second, the prayers of Aidan, in retreat on Farne Island, save the royal fortress at Bamburgh from an attack by Penda, the pagan Mercian ruler. The Northumbrian royal family is saved to continue God's work. Finally, Aidan died while on a preaching mission on a royal estate by Bamburgh. He died lying against a wooden buttress of a church; this buttress later survived a serious fire during another of Penda's raids, and came to be venerated as a relic of the saint through which miracles were worked. Thus, the simple and ascetic bishop was a 'buttress' to the royal power that enabled his mission.

Religious faith and practice and political power were closely entwined; there was no sharp division between the religious and the secular. Faith, whether Christian or pagan, informed the decisions of rulers, and the political world affected faith. The possession of powerful relics, including especially the body of a saint, gave power in both these spheres to those who possessed them.

The Lindisfarne monks undertook, says Rollason, 'some skilled relic-management'.[27] The raising of his body above ground in 698 was in itself a promotion of Cuthbert as a saint, as was the preservation of several items—the chasuble, shoes, and hair—from the original burial. The tomb would have been surrounded by candles and probably covered with precious cloths. Treasures were added to the shrine too—the incised wooden coffin in which Cuthbert's body was placed in 698, the simple portable wooden altar, now encased in silver, and, most spectacular of all, the Lindisfarne Gospels.

According to a tenth-century addition, this magnificent book was made by Eadfrith, bishop of Lindisfarne from 698 to 721, 'in honour of God and of St Cuthbert'. His successor, Ethelwald, was responsible for the binding, which was ornamented with gold, gems and silver-gilt by Billfrith, an anchorite. As the work of one man, this one book probably represents five to ten years of work, and an entire herd of around 130 cattle to provide the vellum. As well as being a beautiful work of art, it also makes a powerful statement about the importance of the saint in whose honour it was made, and at whose shrine it would have been displayed. It was an offering of many years' work, and in itself an act of prayer and sacrifice. Most people who saw the book would not have been able to read it, so the 15 illuminated pages that punctuate the book would have been especially important for these pilgrims. The pictures of the evangelists that precede their Gospels were particularly significant as representing the living word of God. Pilgrims not only looked at the book but experienced the book as looking back at them—as does anyone praying with an icon. These pictures are icons and hence much more than mere decoration.

The pages of pure decoration, loosely based on the form of a cross, which follow the icons of the evangelists, draw on a wide range of motifs and artistic styles from many parts of the known world. The Gospel text is taken from an Italian book, some of the iconography reflects Greek practice, and Irish and Germanic motifs mingle in the ornamentation. Wherever pilgrims came from, they could see in this book something of their own culture, integrated with much that was strange. The book thus made a powerful statement about the overarching Christian presence in every culture. This faith was not confined to one country or language group—it encompassed the whole world.

It is not surprising, therefore, that when the monks finally left Lindisfarne, they took with them, along with the body of Cuthbert and his relics, the Gospels. They first fled in 794, when the Vikings returned who had raided the Northumbrian coast, including Lindisfarne, the year before. Moving down the coast, the Vikings arrived at Jarrow, where they were caught and wiped out. The monks were thus able to return to Lindisfarne, where they found that although the monastery itself had been plundered, the tomb of Cuthbert was untouched—another proof of the saint's power. Vikings had not been driven away entirely, however. They continued to cause trouble, and it may have been in response to this threat that Cuthbert's body was taken to Norham on the River Tweed for a time by Ecgred, bishop of Lindisfarne from 830 to 845. It seems to have been returned to the island, but finally, in 875, the Vikings returned in strength. This time they began their raids further south, so the monks had warning of their approach. They chose to abandon Lindisfarne, in order to save what was more valuable—Cuthbert's body and relics, the relics of some other saints, including Aidan, Oswald and Eata, and the Gospels.

For seven years they wandered around the north of England, and even tried to travel to Ireland, setting sail from the mouth of the River Derwent in Cumbria. But the saint disapproved: a storm blew up, the waves that washed into the boat turned to blood, and the Gospels were washed overboard. Cuthbert was still very active in his own cause. The monks turned back and set out along the coast, hoping to find their precious book. Eventually, at Withern in Galloway, they found it, stranded by the spring tide three miles above the normal high-water mark. Although in the sources for these stories the monks are presented as few and poor, as refugees fleeing the threat of violence, in fact the community had estates all over the north of England, and much of their wandering might in reality have been more of a progress from one estate to another. Grants of land were made to Cuthbert while he was alive and carried on in exactly the same way after his death. The wording of these grants is exactly the same: 'present in his body and in heaven, the dead St Cuthbert was as capable a recipient of gifts as the living one'.[28]

The monks were certainly not averse to wielding political influence. While staying at Crayke in Yorkshire, the abbot had a vision of St Cuthbert telling him to ransom Guthred, the son of Harthacnut, a Dane (and hence linked to the Vikings who had caused their wanderings), and make him king of Northumbria. This they did, and in gratitude the new king settled the monks at Chester-le-Street, building them a fine church and a rich shrine for Cuthbert. In another vision, the saint commanded the king, through the abbot, to give his community all the lands between the Tyne and the Wear. Pilgrims continued to visit Cuthbert's shrine at Chester-le-Street, and many brought rich gifts. King Athelstan, who visited it on his way to Scotland in 933, presented Gospel books, splendid vestments, two gold and silver horns, and two bracelets of gold, among other gifts.

The presentation of the wandering years is probably intended to evoke comparison with Moses leading the Israelites through the wilderness to the promised land, but the reality was undoubtedly far more complex. The equation of Cuthbert with Moses, however, is a powerful one, and certainly he continued to exercise power and even leadership through visions, dreams and miraculous happenings. One of these led to the community's final settlement in Durham.

In 995, after 110 years in Chester-le-Street, the community was again threatened by Viking attack, and moved to Ripon, further south—a poignant return for Cuthbert to the scene of part of his early monastic life. When the Viking threat had gone, they set out to return to Chester-le-Street, but Cuthbert had other ideas. As they travelled, the cart on which the saint's body was being transported became immovable. Bishop Ealdhun ordered a three-day fast and vigil, to find out what the saint wanted. A man named Eadmer received a revelation that Cuthbert wished to rest in Durham, so the community took him there. They made a shelter of boughs to protect the coffin, and then built a wooden church to house the saint, but this too was only intended to be temporary, and a stone cathedral, taking three years to build, was created.

Pilgrims continued to come to Cuthbert's new resting place, and more relics were collected to increase the power of the shrine, including the bones of the Venerable Bede from Jarrow. Even this church lasted only about a century, however. The second Norman bishop of Durham, William Carileph, expelled the English monks, the descendants of the Lindisfarne community, and brought in Benedictine monks. He was ambitious for his diocese and wanted to make the most of having such a powerful saint, so he pulled down the Saxon cathedral and in 1093 began to build a new Norman one. In 1104, when the cathedral was largely completed, Cuthbert's body was moved, with great ceremony, to a new shrine in the apse behind the high altar.

Those who had gathered for this ceremony, including abbots, royalty and bishops, speculated on whether the body could still be intact. So the monks, to allay any doubts, again opened the coffin. They prepared themselves with fasting and prayer, and then, on the night of 24 August, they opened first the outer coffin and then the inner one. They were met with a sweet fragrance and the sight of Cuthbert's body, still fresh and whole, lying on its right side and looking asleep rather than dead. The relics of many other saints were with him in the coffin. They took the body out of the coffin and removed most of the other relics, then replaced the body and put the coffin back into the shrine. When they reported these marvels to the visiting dignitaries the next day, some were still doubtful because all the witnesses had been monks, so they were prevailed upon, with great reluctance, to open the coffin again, this time in the presence of outside witnesses. Only the Abbot of Seez, Ralph d'Escures, was allowed to touch the body, and the monks watched closely to ensure that nothing was taken from the coffin—relics were too valuable to be allowed out of their control. This time all were convinced, and the ceremony went ahead with great pomp and demonstrations of the saint's power in further miraculous happenings. The Abbot of St Albans was miraculously healed; the timberwork supporting the vaulting of the new shrine collapsed just before the body was due to be enshrined, but without harming either the building or the pavement; and a torrential deluge that interrupted an over-long sermon by Ranulph Flambard, bishop of Durham, did no harm to any of the church's treasures which had been caught in it.

At this time, the shrine projected from the east end of the cathedral: the chapel of the Nine Altars which now surrounds it was built in the mid-13th century, and the shrine itself was rebuilt and the screen between the high altar and the tomb erected in the 14th century. It was one of the main centres of pilgrimage in England, and the gifts bestowed on it reflected its importance. In 1383, the then keeper of the shrine, Richard de Segbruk, made a list of all the items in his care. Besides many books, vessels and fabrics, there was the banner of St Cuthbert, containing a piece of fabric which had once been on the saint's body, and huge numbers of relics, reflecting the insatiable craving of the Middle Ages for such things. Among the less probable were 'a part of the tree under which Abraham met the three angels, a piece of the tree of Paradise, a piece of the rod of Moses, something of the sepulchre and chemise of our Lady'[29]—altogether 'a vast hoard of the priceless, the trivial, and the near blasphemous, all brought, at one time or another, to increase the glory of St Cuthbert and his shrine'.[30]

Although the ways of expressing this desire may seem strange to us, there is no mistaking the devotion behind it. An account written in the late 16th century, when the Reformation had swept away the riches of the shrine, give a picture of how it had been earlier that century, and why it was so important. The author describes the four seats where the sick might kneel or lean to pray to St Cuthbert for healing:

…in time of theire devout offeringes and fervent prayers to God and holy Saint Cuthbert for his miraculous releife and succour, which beinge never wantinge, made the Shrine to bee so richly invested, that it was estimated to bee one of the most sumptuous monuments in all England; so great were the offerings and jeweles that were bestowed upon it, and no lesse the miracles that were done by it.[31]

Pilgrims came not simply to pay their respects to a holy man from the past (and, by the time of the Reformation, Cuthbert had been dead for over 800 years), but to ask his help in their present need.

When Henry VIII's commissioners came to Durham Cathedral, they first took away all the items that the jewellers who accompanied them thought valuable, and then began to break up the tomb itself. Expecting to find only bones, they were taken aback to find an intact body. Cuthbert's body was taken out and left for a time in one of the vestries before being reburied in the place where the shrine had stood, under a blue marble slab. The bill for doing this is still among the Cathedral archives.

Today the shrine is still there, on the same spot, and Cuthbert rests under the same plain blue slab, decorated simply with his name. Two modern batik banners, one of Cuthbert and one of Oswald, are the only splashes of colour. It is a far cry from the opulence of its medieval heyday, but perhaps more fitting to the saint who craved a simple life of solitude on Farne. Although pilgrimage is not as popular now as it was then, many people still come, most perhaps from curiosity rather than devotion, but some drawn still by the power of the saint of Lindisfarne. I can only speak for myself, but I have felt him powerfully present there still, and for me that shrine is still holy ground. There is no way that I can step into the cathedral and not be drawn up the aisle to it again, as I was in my initial experience; and even passing through Durham on the train I have to fight a strong impulse to jump off and make my way through the narrow streets up to the cathedral to meet the saint at his shrine.

That sense of real connection with one of God's saints is, for me, one of Cuthbert's most precious gifts. As with all God's gifts, it comes through relationship. God calls us into relationship with him and with his world, and as relationships are individual, so the gifts of relationship will be different for each person, but I think there are some more general gifts that Cuthbert brings—a legacy of his life and his cult that can speak to us today, challenge and encourage us.

He was a unifier, a man with a concern to take the best from the various Christian traditions that met in Northumbria and use them in the service of Christ and of God's people. He did not allow himself to be confined to either the Celtic or the Anglo-Saxon traditions, or to be enlisted on the side of one or the other. At a time when the church seems to divide all-too-readily into opposing parties, each believing that they have a monopoly on the truth, that is a valuable and much-needed example and gift.

The concern for balance extended into his own life, too. Although it was undoubtedly costly, he held together the life of a monk and a missionary, the calling to be a hermit with the church's calling of him as a bishop. The rhythm of time in the monastery was balanced with time outside preaching the word; the solitude of Farne, given to prayer and spiritual warfare, fuelled his short time as a bishop, given to public activity and political involvement. The secular and the religious were held together, and he could as easily minister to kings, queens and princes as to the poor people of the hills round Melrose. All that he did came from a single-minded desire to follow Christ, and so, although he may have had preferences (we know that he craved the solitude of the hermit life), he was able to do what he was asked to do with a grace that shines through in the accounts of his life.

He lived at a time of some conflict and controversy in the church, and perhaps that can be a useful reminder that there never was a time when all Christians were in perfect agreement. Gifts of discernment and choice, and a willingness to believe in the goodwill of others even while disagreeing with their actions, have always been necessary. It never was simple! That recognition can perhaps, paradoxically, dissolve the sense of distance from one who lived many centuries ago. Although the outer circumstances of Cuthbert's life were very different from ours, the same basic concerns, needs and opportunities shaped his days. People still found it difficult to live together harmoniously; they sought healing of mind and body; they were drawn to those who seemed to be in tune with God; they rejoiced in birth and love, and wept at loss and death. Beyond the differences in language, politics, church organization and practice, even food and dress, we can discern the same human struggles with the same human questions.

Coming to know Cuthbert can give us a way into this time and place, and a means of recognizing ourselves in it, so drawing on more of the resources of Christian tradition.

Cuthbert's continuing power after his death, the cult that grew up around him, and the many places associated with him, introduce us to the idea of pilgrimage and holy places. The fact that people travelled from all parts of Britain, and even beyond, at a time when travel was far slower and more arduous than today, gives us some idea of the power of the particular—whether person or place—in the spiritual life. Of course God is everywhere present, and our prayers will be heard wherever we pray, but there is a particular power in the places where, as T.S. Eliot says, 'prayer has been valid'.[32] The act of making the effort to go to a sacred place is in itself a form of prayer, and seems to open us up to God's grace in a particular way. After all, going to visit our friends is a way of sustaining our relationship with them; telephone calls, e-mails and letters can go a long way, but there is no substitute for the face-to-face meeting, the simply spending time in each other's presence, which a visit makes possible. For me, that is part of the value of visiting Lindisfarne and Durham, of standing quietly above the site of the monastery at Melrose and reflecting on Cuthbert's life there. These places are still, after all these centuries, charged with a special touch of God through Cuthbert's life and death, and this special touch is still available to those who come as pilgrims. Cuthbert is not only a long-dead saint but an icon of Christ and a living friend of God, who offers us the chance to share more deeply in that friendship through our relationship with him.

***

BIBLIOGRAPHY AND
FURTHER READING

David Adam, *Holy Island* (Canterbury Press, 1997) (Pilgrimage guide)

Janet Backhouse, *The Lindisfarne Gospels* (The British Library, 1995)

Bede, *A History of the English Church and People* (Penguin, 1990)

Bede, 'Life of Cuthbert', in *The Age of Bede* translated by J.F. Webb (Penguin, 1965)

Peter Hunter Blair, *Northumbria in the Age of Bede* (Llanerch Press, 1997)

Peter Hunter Blair, *The World of Bede* (Cambridge University Press, 1990)

Gerald Bonner et al (eds.), *St Cuthbert, His Cult and His Community to AD1200* (Boydell Press, 1989)

Michelle P. Brown, *Painted Labyrinth: the World of the Lindisfarne Gospels* (The British Library, 2003)

Bertrand Colgrave (ed.), *Two Lives of St Cuthbert* (Cambridge University Press, 1940). Contains the Anonymous Life; is now out of print, but is available through libraries

Ronald Coppin, *Durham* (Canterbury Press, 1997) (Pilgrimage guide)

Douglas Dales, *Light to the Isles: Missionary Theology in Celtic and Anglo-Saxon Britain* (Lutterworth Press, 1998)

Kathleen Hughes and Ann Hamlin, *Celtic Monasticism: the Modern Traveller to the Early Irish Church* (Seabury Press, 1981). Out of print, but should be available through your local library

Michael Lapidge et al, *Blackwell Encyclopaedia of Anglo-Saxon England* (Blackwell, 2000)

Henry Mayr-Harting, *The Coming of Christianity to Anglo-Saxon England* (Penn State University, 3rd edition, 1991)

Benedicta Ward, *High King of Heaven: Aspects of Early English Spirituality* (Mowbray, 1999)

* * *

NOTES

CHAPTER 1

1   David L. Edwards, *Christian England Volume 1: Its story to the Reformation* (Fount, 1981), p. 85

2   D.W. Rollason, 'The Wanderings of St Cuthbert' in *Cuthbert—Saint and Patron*, ed. D.W. Rollason (Dean and Chapter, 1987), p. 53

3   Victoria Tudor, 'The Misogyny of Saint Cuthbert', *Archaeologia Aeliana*, 5, XII, p. 157

4   Bede, 'Life of Cuthbert' chapter 1, in *The Age of Bede*, trans. J.F. Webb (Penguin, 1965), p. 45 (referred to after this as VP, with number indicating chapter number)

5   W.G. Allen, *The Monks of Melrose: Lectures on Early Border Church History* (James Thin, 1892), pp. 19–20

6   VP 9

7   VP 22

8   VP 16

9   VP 16

10 Peter Hunter Blair, *The World of Bede* (Secker and Warburg, 1970), p. 253

11 Anonymous 'Life of St Cuthbert', in *Two Lives of St Cuthbert*, ed. Bertram Colgrave (Cambridge University Press, 1940), I:1 (referred to after this as VA)

CHAPTER 2

1   VP 5

2   VP 15

3   VP 23

4   VP 29

5   VP 35

6   Benedicta Ward, 'The Spirituality of St Cuthbert' in *Signs and Wonders: Saints, Miracles and Prayers from the Fourth Century to the Fourteenth* (Variorum, 1992), pp. 65–76

7   VP Prologue

8   Colgrave, *Two Lives of St Cuthbert*, p. 5

9   Colgrave, *Two Lives of St Cuthbert*, p. 13

10   VP Prologue

11   Charles W. Jones, *Saints' Lives and Chronicles in Early England* (Archon Books, 1967), p. 58

12   Ward, 'The Spirituality of St Cuthbert', pp. 67–68

13   Benedicta Ward, *High King of Heaven: Aspects of Early English Spirituality* (Mowbray, 1999), p. 57

14   Douglas Dales, *Light to the Isles* (Lutterworth, 1997), p. 110

15   Ward, 'The Spirituality of St Cuthbert', p. 72

16   Dales, *Light to the Isles*, p. 10

17   VA III.7; Gerald Bonner, 'Saint Cuthbert—Soul Friend' in *Church and Faith in the Patristic Tradition: Augustine, Pelagianism and Early Christian Northumbria* (Variorum, 1996), pp. 23–42, p. 26

18   VP 8

19   Bede, *A History of the English Church and People*, III:25 (Penguin, 1955) (referred to after this as HE)

20   Bonner, 'Saint Cuthbert—Soul Friend', p. 30

21   J. Campbell, 'Elements in the Background to the Life of St Cuthbert and His Early Cult' in Gerald Bonner et al (eds.), *St Cuthbert, His Cult and His Community to AD1200* (Boydell Press, 1989), pp. 3–19, p. 19

CHAPTER 3

1   VA IV:I

2   VP 8

3   VP 24
4   HE III:17
5   HE III:17
6   W.C. Sellar and R.J. Yeatman, *1066 and All That* (Methuen, 1984), p. 71
7   HE III:25
8   HE III:25
9   Ward, *High King of Heaven*, p. 17
10 VP 16

CHAPTER 4

1   VP 16
2   'The Anonymous History of Abbot Ceolfrith' in Farmer (ed.), *The Age of Bede*, pp. 213–229, p. 216
3   VA III:1
4   Bede, 'Lives of the Abbots of Wearmouth and Jarrow' in Farmer (ed.), *The Age of Bede*, pp. 187–210, p. 198
5   Bede, 'Lives of the Abbots of Wearmouth and Jarrow' in Farmer (ed.), *The Age of Bede*, p. 195
6   'The Anonymous History of Abbot Ceolfrith' in Farmer (ed.), *The Age of Bede*, p. 214
7   VP 18
8   VP 29
9   Kathleen Hughes and Ann Hamlin, *Celtic Monasticism: the Modern Traveller to the Early Irish Church* (Seabury Press, 1981), p. 28
10 VP 9
11 VA II:7
12 VP 14
13 VP 10; the parallel story is in VA II:3
14 VP 37
15 'A Beautiful Friendship Ruined: Bede's Revisionist Writing of Aelffled in the *Life of Cuthbert*' in Stephanie Hollis, *Anglo-Saxon*

Women and the Church (Boydell Press, 1992), pp. 179–207, pp. 185–86

16 VA IV:10

17 VP 34

18 Virginia Tudor, 'The Misogyny of Saint Cuthbert', *Archaeologia Aeliana* 5 XII (1984), pp. 157–167, pp. 158–59

CHAPTER 5

1   VP 4

2   VA I:5

3   VA I:4

4   VA III:1

5   VA IV:1

6   Psalm 34:6

7   VP 11

8   Bede, 'Lives of the Abbots of Wearmouth and Jarrow' in Farmer (ed.), *The Age of Bede*, p. 193

9   VP 17

10 Quoted in Blair, *The World of Bede*, p. 142

11 VP 46

12 VP 20

13 VP 20

14 Hughes and Hamlin, *Celtic Monasticism*, p. 3

15 VP 21

16 VP 22

17 VA III:7

18 VP 22

19 VP 22

CHAPTER 6

1   VP 3

2   HE III:30

3   VP 9
4   Ward, *High King of Heaven*, p. 6
5   Gregory the Great, *Dialogues* iii, 17, quoted in Jones, *Saints' Lives and Chronicles in Early England*, p. 77
6   HE II:13
7   HE II:9
8   VA IV:7
9   VP 33
10 VP 27
11 HE II:14
12 Quoted in Gerald Bonner, 'Anglo-Saxon Culture and Spirituality' in *Church and Faith in the Patristic Tradition*, pp. 533–50, pp. 538–39
13 Margaret Gallyon, *The Early Church in Northumbria* (Terence Dalton, 1977), p. 99
14 Peter Hunter Blair, *Northumbria in the Days of Bede* (Book Club Associates, 1976), p. 108

CHAPTER 7

1   Quoted in Dales, *Light to the Isles*, p. 77
2   VA I:4; VP 2
3   VA II:2; VP 7
4   VA II:5; VP 12
5   VA I:6; VP 5
6   VP 8
7   VP 18
8   VP 17
9   VA III:2
10 VA I:4
11 VP 23
12 VP 31
13 VP 31
14 VP 15

15 VP 27

16 VP 27

17 VP 28

18 VP 36

19 VP 39

20 VP 40

21 VP 37

22 HE IV.31

23 VP 45

24 VP 42

25 I owe these points to D.W. Rollason, 'Why Was St Cuthbert So Popular?' in D.W. Rollason, *Cuthbert—Saint and Patron* (Durham Dean and Chapter, 1987), pp. 11–13

26 Rollason, *Cuthbert—Saint and Patron*, p. 13

27 Rollason, *Cuthbert—Saint and Patron*, p. 18

28 Rollason, 'The Wanderings of St Cuthbert' in Rollason, *Cuthbert—Saint and Patron*, p. 54

29 C.J. Stranks, *The Life and Death of St Cuthbert* (SPCK, 1964), p. 41

30 Stranks, *The Life and Death of St Cuthbert*, p. 41

31 *The Rites of Durham*, Surtees Society (15), 1842, p. 3

32 T.S Eliot, 'Little Gidding I', *Four Quartets*

You may be interested to know that Helen Julian CSF is a regular contributor to *New Daylight*, BRF's popular series of Bible reading notes. Each issue covers four months of daily Bible reading and reflection with each day offering a Bible passage (text included), helpful comment and a prayer or thought for the day ahead.

New Daylight is written by a gifted team of contributors, also including Adrian Plass, David Winter, Gordon Giles, Rachel Boulding, Peter Graves, David Spriggs, Margaret Silf, Jenny Robertson and Veronica Zundel.

New Daylight is also available in large print and on cassette for the visually impaired.

NEW DAYLIGHT SUBSCRIPTIONS

❏ I would like to give a gift subscription
(please complete both name and address sections below)
❏ I would like to take out a subscription myself
(complete name and address details only once)

This completed coupon should be sent with appropriate payment to BRF. Alternatively, please write to us quoting your name, address, the subscription you would like for either yourself or a friend (with their name and address), the start date and credit card number, expiry date and signature if paying by credit card.

Gift subscription name _____

Gift subscription address _____

_____ Postcode _____

Please send to the above, beginning with the next January/May/September issue: (delete as applicable)

(please tick box)	UK	SURFACE	AIR MAIL
NEW DAYLIGHT	❏ £11.40	❏ £12.75	❏ £15.00
NEW DAYLIGHT 3-year sub	❏ £28.95		

Please complete the payment details below and send your coupon, with appropriate payment to: **BRF, First Floor, Elsfield Hall, 15–17 Elsfield Way, Oxford OX2 8FG**

Your name _____

Your address _____

_____ Postcode _____

Total enclosed £ _____ (cheques should be made payable to 'BRF')

Payment by cheque ❏ postal order ❏ Visa ❏ Mastercard ❏ Switch ❏

Card number: ⬚⬚⬚⬚⬚⬚⬚⬚⬚⬚⬚⬚⬚⬚⬚⬚⬚⬚⬚⬚

Expiry date of card: ⬚⬚⬚⬚ Issue number (Switch): ⬚⬚⬚⬚

Signature (essential if paying by credit/Switch card)_____

❏ Please do not send me further information about BRF publicaations.

NB: BRF notes are also available from your local Christian bookshop. **BRF is a Registered Charity**

LIVING THE GOSPEL

THE SPIRITUALITY OF ST FRANCIS AND ST CLARE

Finding freedom in simplicity and voluntary poverty, living in harmony with creation, seeking to be a brother to everyone and everything—so much of the teaching of St Francis directly challenges the values of today's consumer-driven culture, providing a radical, liberating alternative. Yet while he remains an enduringly popular figure in the history of Christian spirituality, St Clare, an early follower and teacher of his values, is far less well-known. *Living the Gospel* looks at St Francis and St Clare together, showing how they shared responsibility for the growth and influence of the Franciscan order, and how deeply rooted their teaching was in Scripture.

This book is ideal for people already interested in the teaching of St Francis as well as those whose explorations have extended no further than singing 'All creatures of our God and King'—a version of Francis' *Canticle of the Creatures*. And it introduces St Clare to a wider audience—a comparatively little-known but surprisingly influential female spiritual leader.

ISBN 1 84101 126 6   £5.99
Available from your local Christian bookshop or direct from BRF using the form overleaf.

ORDER FORM

REF	TITLE	PRICE	QTY	TOTAL
126 6	*Living the Gospel*	£5.99		

POSTAGE AND PACKING CHARGES					
order value	UK	Europe	Surface	Air Mail	
£7.00 & under	£1.25	£3.00	£3.50	£5.50	
£7.01–£30.00	£2.25	£5.50	£6.50	£10.00	
Over £30.00	free	prices on request			

Postage and packing:

Donation:

Total enclosed:

Name _____ Account Number _____

Address _____

_____ Postcode _____

Telephone Number _____ Email _____

Payment by: Cheque ❏ Mastercard ❏ Visa ❏ Postal Order ❏ Switch ❏

Credit card no. ❏❏❏❏ ❏❏❏❏ ❏❏❏❏ ❏❏❏❏   Expires ❏❏ ❏❏

Switch card no. ❏❏❏❏❏❏❏❏❏❏❏❏❏❏❏❏❏❏

Issue no. of Switch card ❏❏❏❏   Expires ❏❏ ❏❏

Signature _____ Date _____

All orders must be accompanied by the appropriate payment.

Please send your completed order form to:
BRF, First Floor, Elsfield Hall, 15–17 Elsfield Way, Oxford OX2 8FG
Tel. 01865 319700 / Fax. 01865 319701 Email: enquiries@brf.org.uk

❏ Please send me further information about BRF publications.

Available from your local Christian bookshop.   BRF is a Registered Charity